100+ recipes inside!

KETO 2.0

APPROVED

Low Carb, **High** Gains.
All the **benefits**, less **restrictions**.

More options than any other keto diet!
The perfect choice for anyone who was previously scared off by the limitations of the classic keto diet.

Effie Manolas

To all the people who are struggling on their weight loss journey. I hope this new Keto 2.0 diet – with more benefits and less restrictions – will help you achieve all your goals.

Copyright © 2022 Effie Manolas.
All rights reserved.

No part of this book may be reproduced or used in any manner without the prior written permission of the author.

DISCLAIMER

The purpose of this book is to provide information only. The information is NOT a substitution for medical, psychological, or professional advice, diagnosis, or treatment. The author recommends that you seek the advice of your physician or other qualified health care provider to present them with questions you may have regarding any medical condition. Advice from your trusted, professional medical advisor should always supersede the information presented in this book.

CONTENTS

Introduction	01
All about **fat**	11
Ketosis and **fasting**	13
Is it right **for me**?	15
Summary	167

SEE NEXT PAGE FOR **RECIPE** INDEX

KETO 2.0 RECIPES

Breakfast & Eggs   18

Pancakes................................ 19	Pumpkin Muffins...................... 24
Almond Flour Crepes............. 20	Strawberry Oatmeal................ 25
Sesame Seed Bagels............. 21	Breakfast Casserole................ 26
Banana Bread......................... 22	Egg stuffed Avocado.............. 27
Blueberry Muffins................... 23	Egg Salad................................ 29

Appetizers & Snacks   30

Pickles 31	Cheesy Chicken Quesadillas.... 36
Zucchini fries......................... 32	Cheese Sticks......................... 38
Avocado fries........................ 33	Onion Rings............................ 40
Tuna Cucumber Boats........... 35	Chips - 4 Ways....................... 42
	Stuffed Bell Peppers............... 44

Salads & Soups   46

Egg Drop Soup...................... 47	Clam Chowder........................ 52
Lobster Bisque...................... 48	Dill Cucumber Onion Salad..... 54
Chicken, Shrimp & Sausage Gumbo 50	Cobb Salad............................. 55
	Broccoli Cheddar Soup........... 57

Vegan   58

Sauteed Mushrooms............. 59	Grilled Eggplant...................... 62
Buffalo Cauliflower Wings..... 61	Pesto Zucchini Noodles......... 63

KETO 2.0 RECIPES

Vegetable Sides — 65

Cauliflower Rice 66	Garlic Roasted Bok Choy 71
Cauliflower Fried Rice 67	Sriracha Brussels Sprouts 72
Mashed Cauliflower 69	Jicama Fries 73
Spicy Asparagus 70	Spaghetti Squash with Bacon 74
	Fried Cabbage with Bacon 75

Poultry — 76

Chicken Salad Lettuce Wrap 77	Chicken Thighs 83
Chicken Souvlaki Skewers 78	Chicken Piccata 85
Creamy Tuscan Chicken 79	Chicken Nuggets 87
Chicken & Broccoli Casserole 80	Baked Chicken Wings 89
Marinated Chicken Drumsticks 81	Honey Soy Duck Breast 90

Beef & Lamb — 91

Chili 92	Mongolian Beef 99
Beef Tamales 93	Meatloaf 101
Beef Jerky 95	Beef Enchiladas 103
Corned Beef Cabbage 96	Chimichurri Flank Steak 105
Beef Stroganoff 97	Fajitas 107

Pork — 108

BBQ Ribs 109	Pigs in a Blanket 114
Carnitas 111	Pork Tenderloin 115
Cheesy Sausage Meatballs 113	Pulled Pork 116

KETO 2.0 RECIPES

Fish & Seafood — 117

Tuna Tartare 118	Lemon Salmon 126
Fried Oysters 119	Avocado Salmon Sushi 127
Shrimp Pad Thai 120	Crab Cakes 128
Alfredo Shrimp Pasta 122	Crab Dip 129
Shrimp Skewers 124	Bacon-Wrapped Scallops 130
Coconut Shrimp 125	Crab & Bacon Stuffed Mushrooms ... 131

Dips & Sauces — 132

Queso 2.0 133	Ketchup 137	Alfredo Sauce 141
Guacamole 134	Mayonnaise 138	Tzatziki 142
Spinach Dip 135	Barbeque Sauce . 139	Ranch 143
Salsa 136	Nutella 140	Dill Veggie Dip 144

Sweets & Deserts — 145

Chocolate Cake 146	Strawberry Shortcake 152
Brownies 148	Chocolate Almond Protein Bars ... 153
Banana Chai Pudding 149	No-Bake Lemmon Posset Tart ... 154
Crème Caramel 150	Lemon Cheesecake 156
	(Mint) Cookie Dough Ice Cream ... 158

Smoothies & Beverages — 159

Bullet Proof Coffee 160	Vanilla Protein Shake 163
Chocolate Shake 161	Blueberry Shake 164
Strawberry Vanilla Shake 162	Cinnamon Shake 165
	Spinach Green Smoothie 166

01 Introduction

At this point in time, most people are familiar with the ketogenic diet - or keto for short. Over the past few years, it's become popular among people looking to lose weight, as well as those who want to perform at their best, mentally and physically.

The keto diet is typically high in fat and moderate in protein. That combined with minimizing carbs encourages your body to enter a state called "ketosis", where you switch from using carbohydrate stores to fat stores as your main source of energy.

Until recently, there have been 5 main types of keto diets. These diets are determined by the macronutrient ratio, with some variations allowing more flexibility than others.

Classic Keto Diet

All keto diets share low-carb and high-fat guidelines, but the classic keto diet is arguably the most strict (and therefore more challenging to maintain). This low carb diet can be challenging because very few people truly understand what a carb really is, the foods that contain them, and how much they are currently eating!

90% FAT   **6% PROTEIN**   **4% CARBS**

Targeted Keto Diet; (TKD)

A targeted Ketogenic Diet is sometimes referred to as the Classic Keto diet's sister. This variation is most popular with athletes and active individuals because it allows an additional 20-30 grams of carbs immediately before and after workouts. Those who need more carbs per day for energy often opt for this diet.

*more carbs on exercise days

65% FAT (65-75%)   **20% PROTEIN**   **15% CARBS*** (10-15%)

Standard Keto Diet; (SKD)

With SKD you will eat less than 50 grams of carbs per day. If you're not careful, even small amounts of sugar can throw your body into ketosis. You also want to keep your protein intake to no more than 4g per day; high amounts of protein can decrease blood glucose levels which can hinder your ability to achieve ketosis.

70% FAT   **20% PROTEIN**   **10% CARBS**

Cyclical Keto Diet; (CKD)

CKD is quite different from the other variations, as it requires five days of low carbs and two days of high carbs. This keeps your body from entering ketosis too often. It also allows for more flexibility but it can come at the cost of slower results (especially for weight loss).

*macros for high-carb days: **60% FAT**   **25% PROTEIN**   **15% CARBS**

High Protein Keto Diet; (HPKD)

This diet is often considered an easier entry point into the keto lifestyle because it is not as restrictive as others. It is similar to the classic keto diet but incorporates more protein. Protein is a great source of energy and helps to build muscle tissue.

60% FAT   **35% PROTEIN**   **5% CARBS**

And now, without further ado...

Keto 2.0; (K2)

Keto 2.0 is a more flexible version of the original keto diet; you still get all the benefits with fewer restrictions. There are more options for your meals and snacks than any other keto diet! It's the perfect choice for anyone who was previously scared off by the limitations of the classic keto diet.

50% FAT **30% PROTEIN** **20% CARBS**

In a K2 diet, the proposed macros shift to 50% fat, 20% carb, and 30% protein. Unlike the classic keto diet, these macro recommendations are much more flexible, and act as guidelines than strict rules.

With more flexibility and fewer restrictions, K2 is becoming increasingly popular among vegetarians (and even some creative vegans!). There is more of an emphasis placed on healthy fats and vegetables in addition to your animal products like meat, fish and eggs (with small amounts of dairy). This makes Keto 2.0 suitable for those who have health issues or are on medications that don't allow them to follow an extremely restrictive diet plan (like the original keto diet).

It can seem confusing at first, and you may have a hard time finding many Keto 2.0 recipes out there... which is exactly why I wrote this book! Not only will I provide you with **over 100 Keto 2.0** recipes to browse, but I also provide you with the information you need to create your own! More importantly, you'll be able to tweak your existing favorites in a way that becomes K2 friendly! Just like any Keto diet, it should be thought of as a lifestyle choice rather than a phase. Especially if you want to maintain the health benefits long term! To summarize, here are the three main differences between Keto 2.0 and traditional Keto diets:

#1 plant-based > animal-based

Keto 2.0 puts more of an emphasis on plant-based nutrients - especially when it comes to fat intake. Avocado, coconut oil, and nuts and seeds are excellent plant-based fats that are high in fiber and water content. This helps keep you hydrated and satiated, so you don't feel like snacking all day!

Some proponents of Keto 2.0 also recommend decreasing the amount of dairy that you eat, such as heavy whipping cream, yogurt, and cheese. The reason is due to the fact that for some, consuming too much dairy can lead to inflammation of the gut, among other issues.

If you are currently eating dairy and have no health issues from doing so, then there is no reason to stop eating it altogether! Just reduce it in ways that make sense for you.

#2 Switch up the protein!

There are plenty of meat and fish options on any keto diet... and Keto 2.0 is all about switching up your protein sources! As for meat protein, you're simply encouraged to limit your red meat intake and favor leaner sources instead, like chicken breasts and fish.

When it comes to **seafood**, K2 focuses more on fatty fish like salmon, sardines, and tuna. These types of fish are high in healthy fats as well as protein without carbs.

Poultry seems to be easier to discern when it comes to lean cuts. For red meat, there are a LOT more options; it can be overwhelming to figure out what the best choices are for you. Below you'll find a list of the leanest options for red meat cuts:

Lean Red Meat Options: (as per the Mayo Clinic)

- Strip steak
  (also known as top loin steak)
- Shoulder steak
  (also known as ranch steak)
- Bottom round roast or steak
  (also known as London broil steak)
- Sirloin steaks
  (specifically top, center-cut roast and tip side)
- Shoulder tender roasts or medallions
- Shoulder or arm pot roasts
- Eye of round roast or steak
- Shank crosscuts

- T-bone steak
- Flank steak
- Brisket flat half steak
- Tenderloin steak
- Tri-tip roast or steak
- Top round roast or steak

Athletes, rest assured, you don't **need** a ton of red meat to fuel you; you can still get plenty of protein through other sources on the K2 diet! It's not about eating only chicken and fish and eliminating red meat altogether; you can still eat it, but choose leaner cuts (like listed above) and limit your portion size.

Not to mention, **there are plenty of non-meat sources that can provide you with protein** on the K2 diet! Eggs are an excellent (eggcellent) source of high-quality protein and contain all nine essential amino acids. As a bonus, eggs are also rich in vitamins A and E, which help promote healthy skin and hair!

Nuts and seeds are another great choice that provide a good amount of protein as well as healthy fats that help keep you full between meals. Nuts and seeds are also high in fiber, which helps keep blood sugars stable. You do, however, have to be careful which nuts and seeds you choose, as certain ones have more carbohydrates per serving.

Here are a list of nuts and seeds to **avoid** when possible:
(or eliminate)

- **Chestnuts** - 17 net carbs per ¼ cup serving

- **Cashews** - 8.5 net carbs per ¼ cup serving

- **Peanuts** - 8 net carbs per ¼ cup serving

- **Pistachios** - 5 net carbs per ¼ cup serving

- **Sunflower seeds** - 4 net carbs per ¼ cup serving

K2 Friendly **Nuts** & **Seeds**

macros per ¼ cup

| PROTEIN | FAT | NET CARBS |

- Flax seeds
  - 5g | 12g | 0.5g

- Macadamia nuts
  - 2g | 21g | 1.3g

- Chia seeds
  - 4g | 9g | 1g

- Pecans
  - 3g | 20g | 2g

- Walnuts
  - 4g | 18g | 2g

- Brazil nuts
  - 4g | 19g | 1g

- Hazelnuts
  - 4g | 17g | 2g

- Almonds
  - 6g | 14g | 3g

- Hemp seeds
  - 6g | 10g | 1g

- Pumpkin seeds
  - 8g | 13g | 2g

# More flexibility with **macros**

While all keto diets require you to stay within certain macronutrient ranges (fats, carbs and proteins), K2 allows more flexibility than others. Rather than counting every single calorie and carb, you can simply focus on eating foods that are high in fat and low in carbs. This makes it easier to follow for many, because there are less restrictions involved in calculating the macros in your meals. The traditional keto diet recommends 5-10% of your daily macronutrients to come from carbohydrates. The K2 guidelines increases it to about 10-20%. These macros are not set in stone like they are on other ketogenic diets. For example, you can tailor your diet to include more protein than a typical keto diet if you are looking to build more muscle mass.

While more carbohydrates are allowed on this diet, the goal is to get them from plant based foods. Plant-based carbohydrates come from the fiber content, which will not spike your glucose level the way some carbs will.

Carbohydrates are sugar molecules that the body converts into energy. Some carbohydrates raise blood sugar more quickly than others; some raise blood sugar less quickly. Both types can cause insulin spikes when consumed in excess. If they aren't being used as energy immediately after eating them (in which case they get stored as glycogen) both types can lead to fat storage. So, while there is more flexibility with macros on the K2 diet, if you're trying to lose weight or otherwise improve your health through dieting, then limiting the number of carbs you consume is a good idea; it makes it easier for your body to break down other macronutrients - especially protein - to be used as fuel, instead of storing them for later use as fat. If you are looking to maximize building muscle mass, try to consume the most carbs during your recovery phase, post-workout.

K2 Friendly Vegetables

macros per 1 cup

PROTEIN | FAT | NET CARBS

As a general rule of thumb, vegetables that grow above ground are lower in carbs, while those growing below the ground (root vegetables) are higher in carbs. Below are some vegetables that may be harder to incorporate on a typical keto diet, but with the K2 macro flexibility, they are more acceptable (easier to incorporate) on a K2 diet:

- Broccoli — 2g | 0.g | 4g
- Brussel sprouts — 3g | 0g | 8g
- Bok Choy — 4g | 0.g | 6g
- Green Beans — 1g | 0.g | 6g
- Zucchini — 1g | 0.g | 3g
- Rutabaga — 1g | 0.g | 12g

02 All about FAT

Any keto diet places a higher focus on **fat** than most diets. The K2 diet is designed to shift your body into fat-burning mode; your body uses fat as its primary fuel source instead of carbohydrates. Some people love the idea of adding more fat to their diet. Others find it difficult to reach the recommended intake. It's important to remember that fat is an essential nutrient! It helps you absorb vitamins, like A, D, E and K. There's one kind of fat that's particularly important: **saturated fat.**

Saturated fat is a source of energy for your body. It also helps protect your heart by lowering your LDL cholesterol (the "bad" kind) and raising HDL cholesterol (the "good" kind). So despite the word have some stigma attached to it, there are a lot of benefits to adding more fat to your diet

(you just have to do it the right way!)

Quality over quantity

The best way to consume fat is by focusing on the **quality**, not the quantity. Choosing the right sources for these fats should be a priority, as some fats are better for you than others (think coconut oil versus saturated fat from processed snacks). **Avocados** are an excellent example of a quality source of fat. They have been shown to provide numerous benefits including improved heart health, bone strength and skin elasticity. While they are quite high in fat (approximately 30 g per whole avocado), they help regulate blood sugar levels and reduce inflammation, which can actually lead to **weight loss**.

Even though this fruit may be high in calories per serving size — an average avocado contains 240 calories — it is rich in healthy monounsaturated fatty acids.

Keto 2.0 also shines the spotlight on other plant-based unsaturated fats like olive oil, nuts, and seeds. Like avocados, these food sources tend to be high in monounsaturated fat, which research shows can support healthy cholesterol levels (lowered LDL and increased HDL) weight management, blood pressure, blood sugar, heart health, and triglycerides.

As a general rule of thumb, saturated and trans fats are considered unhealthy, while unsaturated fats are considered healthy.

In reality, it is not quite so black-and-white. Avocados contain a small amount of saturated fat, but it doesn't mean you avoid them altogether! They are mostly nutritious, so you can enjoy their many benefits in moderation.

03 Ketosis & Fasting

As briefly mentioned before, ketosis is a metabolic state where your body burns fat for energy instead of carbohydrates. It's the process that allows you to lose weight, or maintain a healthy weight, without having to focus only on restricting calories. There are two main ways to get into ketosis:

- Eat less than 30 grams of carbs per day (some people start with 20 grams)
- Fast for at least 12 hours overnight (or until you're out of glycogen - the stored form of carbohydrates in your body)

Some people think that being in ketosis is dangerous because it sounds like "ketoacidosis," but this isn't true at all. When someone with type 1 diabetes has diabetic ketoacidosis (DKA), they have excess ketones circulating in their blood as well as high blood sugar levels—that's what makes it so dangerous! If you have type 2 diabetes, then you probably won't develop DKA unless there is another underlying condition present that causes it to happen (like infection).

In fact, one reason why people with type 2 diabetes may want to try going into ketosis is because many studies have shown that it helps improve insulin sensitivity and lowers A1c levels—which could mean fewer complications down the road! But, of course, **if you have any underlying diagnoses or health concerns, always talk to your doctor before changing up your diet**.

What's the deal with **intermittent fasting?**

For those unaware, **fasting** is the intentional abstinence of food for a specified period of time. Many people who are focused on healthy living practice **intermittent fasting**. The most popular form of intermittent fasting (or **IF**) is the 16:8 method, where you fast for 16 hours and eat within the remaining 8 hour window of your day.

Intermittent fasting is associated with many health benefits, like improved cholesterol levels, weight loss, reduced inflammation and better blood sugar control. But for some, there's one big problem with this kind of dieting - hunger pangs! Depending on the time of day you are fasting, if your body feels hungry you may experience irritability or fatigue. This is exactly why most people choose to use the hours they sleep at night as part of the fasting window. For example, if you eat dinner early and stop eating at around 7:30 pm at night, you can wake up, make your own **bullet proof coffee** for breakfast, drink water throughout the morning and be ready to eat lunch by 11:30.

But, why, or how, does **fasting** help achieve **ketosis**?

When you are fasting, your glycogen stores and insulin levels decrease. As a response, your body begins to shift its fuel source from carbohydrates to burning fat for fuel; **ketosis**! Those who combine intermittent fasting with a K2 diet often experience quicker and more efficient fat loss.

04 Is it right for me?

You may be wondering, "is this diet right for me and my lifestyle?" Maybe you've heard about potential unwanted side effects of the diet, and/or you are skeptical that the results are really as good as people say. The countless benefits that come with a ketogenic diet are undoubtedly great, but it is important to talk about the potential side effects as well.

Have you heard about the dreaded 'keto flu'? While the name is a bit dramatic, it is a real thing and can happen to anyone who decides to begin a ketogenic diet. The symptoms of keto flu include nausea, fatigue, headache, muscle aches and pains, dizziness and irritability. These are all normal symptoms for when your body switches from burning glucose (sugar) for energy to burning ketones instead. For most individuals, these symptom fade within a few weeks of starting their keto diet.

Constipation is another potential side effect of a ketogenic lifestyle, particularly for those who are not consuming enough keto-friendly fruits and vegetables. On the other hand, some people experience diarrhea. Lastly, it is not uncommon for someone following a keto diet to experience bad breath. As your body gets used to breaking down more fat instead of glucose, ketones are released into the blood and pass through the lungs to be expelled from the body. The best way to avoid this side effect is by choosing healthy fats whenever possible.

Ultimately, switching up your diet in any way can cause gastrointestinal... surprises; it's always a good idea to take it slow at first. Start by decreasing your intake of carbohydrates and increasing your intake of fats over the course of several weeks, until you reach your desired ratio. While the side effects can be uncomfortable at first, anyone on a ketogenic diet will tell you that the **pros far outweigh the cons**.

But, I have some great news for you! **With the flexibility of K2 diet, all of these unwanted side effects are far less likely to occur**. If you do get any kind of 'K2 flu' it should cause far less discomfort, especially if you follow the steps above!

Bonus tip: meal prepping can be an excellent tool to use when you start a K2 diet. Plan your meals and snacks ahead of time so you don't have to stress about counting macros at each meal. Try to have a couple K2 friendly snacks you can easily take on the go with you, so you don't fall into temptation if you are out and about without many options.

Who should try a **K2** diet?

The keto 2.0 diet is a great option for people who want to lose weight and improve their health, but the drastic changes involved in the diet make it easy to become overwhelmed by all of the information out there. Here are some questions that can help determine if this could be your next diet breakthrough:

- Do you have high cholesterol?
- Do you struggle with high blood pressure?
- Are you overweight or obese?
- Do you have trouble maintaining weight loss (even on other diets)?
- Do you want to improve your mental health?
- Do you want to improve your physical health?
- Do you want to improve your athletic performance?

If you answered 'yes' to any of the above questions, and there are no concerns from your doctor, then the K2 diet might be the best diet you've ever tried!

And now, without further ado, over **100 K2 friendly recipes** to help you start on your health and wellness journey!

KETO 2.0

APPROVED

Breakfast & Egg Recipes

INGREDIENTS

prep time: 1 min
total time: 10 mins
servings: eight

- **⅓ cup** coconut flour
- **½ tsp** baking powder
- **6 large** egg whites, divided
- **½ cup** milk of choice
- **2 tbsp** Greek yogurt can use sour cream
- **1 tsp** vanilla extract (optional)
- **1 drop** liquid stevia (optional)

Pancakes

DIRECTIONS

- Combine all dry ingredients in a bowl; mix well.
- Add the egg whites one at a time, followed by the remaining ingredients.
- Mix well, until a thick batter forms.
- Grease a non-stick pan and set it down on medium heat.
- The pan is ready for use if you pour a drop or two of water and it immediately sizzles (but too much sizzle means too much heat!).
- When ready, spoon the batter onto the pan and cover it (with a clear lid if possible).
- It should take about 3-4 minutes for the edges start turning golden.
- When you see this, remove the lid, flip the pancake, and cook for another 2-3 minutes.
- Repeat the process for all pancakes, let cool, and top with any K2 friendly fruits you'd like.
- Best served immediately but can be kept in the fridge for 4-5 days (simply pop in the toaster to reheat!).

INGREDIENTS

 prep time: 5 min  total time: 10 mins  servings: four

- **4 large** eggs, room temperature
- **⅓ cup** blanched almond flour
- **2 tbsp** granulated erythritol (or sweetener of choice)
- **1 tsp** vanilla or almond extract
- K2 friendly whipped cream (or alternative), **for serving**
- Fresh mixed berries of your choice, **for serving**
- **1 tsp** butter or cooking spray

Almond Flour Crêpes

DIRECTIONS

- In a medium bowl, whisk the first 4 ingredients together until smooth; don't overmix.
- Set a 10-inch non-stick skillet over medium heat, spraying lightly with cooking oil spray.
- Pour ¼ cup of the crêpe batter onto the skillet, tilting it in a circular motion to evenly coat the cooking surface.
- Cook each crêpe for 90 seconds to 2 minutes, depending on your heat settings, until the edges are golden brown and lifting slightly off the pan.
- Carefully flip, and cook the other side for an additional 1-2 minutes, until golden brown. Repeat until you have finished the batter.
- When serving, fill each crêpe with keto whipped cream and fresh berries (or other desired filling).

INGREDIENTS

 prep time: 5 min    total time: 20 mins   servings: eight

- **1 ¾ cup** almond flour
- **1 tbsp** baking powder
- **3 cups** mozzarella cheese, shredded
- **2 oz** cream cheese softened
- **3 large** eggs, divided
- **1 tbsp** sesame seeds (or toppings of your choice)

Sesame Seed Bagels

DIRECTIONS

- Preheat oven to 400°F.
- Combine the flour and baking powder in a small bowl; set aside.
- Place the mozzarella cheese and cream cheese in a microwave safe bowl and heat in 30 second increments, until the mixture is almost melted. Remove carefully and stir until smooth.
- Place 2 of the eggs, the dry ingredients as well as the melted mixture into a food processor; pulse until smooth.
- Lightly flour a surface with almond flour. Divide the dough into eight equal portions on the floured surface, and roll each portion into thin logs. Curl and connect the 2 sides of each ones to form your bagels.
- Place the bagels onto a large baking tray lined with parchment paper.
- In a small bowl, whisk the last egg and brush onto the tops of each bagel before sprinkling with sesame seeds
- Bake for 12-15 minutes, until golden on top and slightly firm to touch.
- Remove from the oven and let them cool completely, before serving.

INGREDIENTS

prep time: 5 min total time: 10 mins servings: four

- 1 cup coconut flour
- 1 cup almond flour
- 1 tsp baking powder
- ½ tsp baking soda
- 1 tbsp cinnamon
- 2 large bananas
- ½ cup maple syrup
- 1 tsp vanilla extract
- ½ cup coconut oil softened
- 3 large eggs

Banana Bread

VEGETARIAN

DIRECTIONS

- Preheat the oven to 320°F. Lightly oil a loaf pan or line with parchment paper; set aside.
- In a large bowl, add the dry ingredients, mix, and set aside.
- In a separate bowl, combine maple syrup, mashed bananas and vanilla extract; mix until combined.
- In a third (and last) bowl, add the softened coconut oil and eggs and beat until smooth. Stir in the mashed banana mixture.
- Fold the dry ingredients until combined and pour into the pan.
- Bake for 50-55 minutes, or until a fork comes out clean.
- After removing from the oven, let it cool in the pan completely.

This recipe has higher carbs due to the bananas - it would never be allowed on a typical keto diet! Save it for a time when you need the extra carbs, and never eat more than one serving per day.

For a lower carb substitution, you can sub pumpkin puree for the bananas to make pumpkin bread.

HIGHER CARB ALERT

INGREDIENTS

 prep time: 10 min　 total time: 30 mins　 servings: twelve

- 2 ½ **cup** blanched almond flour
- ½ **cup** Besti Monk Fruit Allulose Blend
- 1 ½ **tsp** baking powder
- ¼ **tsp** salt (optional, but recommended)
- ⅓ **cup** coconut oil (measure solid, before melting; can sub butter)
- ⅓ **cup** unsweetened almond milk (room temperature)
- 3 **large** eggs (room temperature)
- ½ **tsp** vanilla extract
- 3/4 **cup** blueberries

Blueberry Muffins

DIRECTIONS

- Preheat the oven to 350°F and line a muffin pan with silicone or parchment paper muffin liners.
- In a large bowl, stir in all dry ingredients.
- Melt the coconut oil, and stir in almond milk, eggs, and vanilla extract.
- Add wet mixture to dry mixture and combine.
- Gently fold in the blueberries.
- Distribute the batter evenly among the muffin cups.
- You can split this recipe into 12 smaller muffins for lower calories/carbs per serving, or 10 larger muffins.
- Bake for about 20-25 minutes, (until the top is golden, and/or a fork or toothpick comes out clean).

INGREDIENTS

 prep time: 10 min
 total time: 35 mins
 servings: ten

- ½ **cup** coconut flour
- ½ **cup** blanched almond flour
- ½ **cup** Besti Monk Fruit Allulose Blend
- 1 **tbsp** baking powder
- 1 **tbsp** pumpkin pie spice
- ¼ **tsp** salt
- 4 large eggs
- ¾ **cup** pumpkin puree
- ½ **cup** unsweetened almond milk
- ½ **cup** ghee (measured solid, then melted; can sub butter or coconut oil)
- 1 **tsp** vanilla extract
- 3 **tbsp** pumpkin seeds

Pumpkin Muffins

DIRECTIONS

- Preheat the oven to 350°F and line a muffin tray with liners.
- In a large bowl, stir together the dry ingredients mix until combined, ensuring there are no clumps.
- Stir the wet ingredients one at a time, until completely incorporated.
- Spoon the batter evenly into the muffin cups and smooth the tops. (They should be almost full, not 2/3 or 3/4 full.) If desired, sprinkle pumpkin seeds on top and press gently.
- Bake for about 25 minutes, or until a toothpick comes out clean.
- When cooked completely the muffins should be slightly golden around the edges.

INGREDIENTS

 prep time: 2 min    total time: 6 mins   servings: one

- 3 **tbsp** almond meal
- 1 **tbsp** coconut flour
- 1 **tsp** ground flax-seed
- 1 **tbsp monk fruit** sweetener (or sweetener of choice)
- 1 **tsp** chia seeds
- small shake of salt
- ⅛ **tsp** cinnamon
- 4 chopped strawberries

Strawberry Oatmeal

Choose your own toppings for this simple oatmeal recipe. You can also make this on the stove by boiling your water first, then adding all of your dry ingredients.

DIRECTIONS

- In a bowl, stir almond meal, coconut flour, ground flax-seed, monk fruit sweetener, chia seeds, cinnamon, and salt. Stir well.
- Add ½ cup boiling water, mix and let stand 2-3 minutes.
- Top with strawberries or other keto 2.0 friendly berries like blueberries or blackberries!
- Plums, cantaloupe and coconut are lower carb non-berry options.

INGREDIENTS

 prep time: 15 min  total time: 50 mins   servings: eight

- **10** large eggs
- **16 oz** breakfast sausage
- **1 cup** bell pepper, chopped
- **¼ cup** red onion, chopped
- **¼ cup** heavy cream
- **½ tsp** salt
- **¼ tsp** black pepper
- **¼ tsp** red pepper flakes
- **1 ½ cups** shredded cheddar cheese blend
- **6** strips of bacon

Breakfast Casserole

DIRECTIONS

- Preheat the oven to 375°F. Spray a 2-quart baking/casserole dish with cooking spray, set aside. Cook bacon as desired, set aside.
- Lightly brown the sausage in a large skillet over medium-high heat.
- Add the bell pepper and onion, and sauté for 3-4 minutes.
- When finished, spread the mixture in evenly on the bottom of the baking dish.
- Whisk the eggs in a small bowl, mix in the heavy cream and season with salt, pepper, and red pepper flakes.
- Pour the egg mixture evenly over the sausage and veggies in the dish.
- Sprinkle with shredded cheese, and crumbled bacon.
- Bake for 25-30 minutes, until the eggs are set and the is cheese bubbling slightly. Remove from the oven and cool before serving.

INGREDIENTS

 prep time: 10 min  total time: 25 mins   servings: two

- **1** large room temperature avocado, (ripe but still firm)
- **2** small eggs
- **½ tsp** salt
- **¼ tsp** freshly ground black pepper
- **¼ tsp** garlic salt
- **¼ tsp** red pepper flakes
- **1 tbsp** chopped parsley
- Bacon strips or crumble, optional

Egg Stuffed Avocado

DIRECTIONS

- Preheat oven to 450 °F. Line a small baking dish with foil or parchment paper.
- Cut the avocado in half lengthwise and carefully remove the pit.
- Use a spoon to scoop out a little of the avocado flesh from each half - scoop enough to accommodate the egg.
- **Tip**: make the whole wider rather than deep; this will help ensure the egg cooks evenly.
- Season the avocado halves with half of the salt, black pepper, garlic salt (or any of your favorite spices).

Continued on next page ->

CONTINUED

- Place the avocado halves facing up in the baking dish; make sure they are propped up or balanced so the egg will not pour over the sides.
- Break each egg into a small bowl, taking caution to keep the yolk intact.
- Pour one egg into the center of each avocado half carefully. Gently use a spoon to help nudge the yolk in.
- Bake for approximately 15 minutes, or until the egg whites are set.
- Season with the remaining salt, freshly ground black pepper, garlic salt, red pepper flakes, and garnish with chopped parsley.
- Add bacon strips or crumbles if desired, and serve immediately.

INGREDIENTS

 prep time: 10 min  total time: 10 mins servings: four

- **6** hard boiled eggs, peeled & chopped
- **3 ½ tbsp** mayonnaise (for homemade mayo recipe see **page 138**)
- **1 tsp** finely chopped red onion
- **1 tbsp** finely chopped pickles (for K2 pickle recipe, **page 31**)
- **¼ tsp** salt
- fresh black pepper, **to taste**
- **⅛ tsp** sweet paprika, for garnish
- chopped chives, **for garnish**

Egg Salad

This egg salad recipe is quick, super easy and delicious; so simple there are only three directions to follow! It is packed with K2 friendly protein and can be easily customized if you are looking for more variety with the flavors. It's perfect for taking to work as a snack... or whenever you need an extra protein boost but don't have time to cook a full meal!

DIRECTIONS

- Combine all the ingredients and refrigerate until ready to eat.
- Serve by itself or as a lettuce or celery 'boat'.

KETO 2.0

APPROVED

Snack & **Appetizer** Recipes

INGREDIENTS

 prep time: 10 min   total time: 1 day   servings: four

- **3** cucumbers (approximately 6 inches)
- **½ cup** apple cider vinegar
- **½ cup** water
- **3** garlic cloves
- **1 tbsp** Besti Powdered Monk Fruit Allulose Blend, or similar
- **¼ cup** fresh dill
- **1 tsp** black peppercorns
- **1 tsp** salt
- **½ tsp** red pepper flakes

Pickles

DIRECTIONS

- Slice the cucumbers in half length wise, and repeat so you have 4 long quarters per cucumber.
- Cut garlic cloves in half, lengthwise. Remove the fresh dill stems.
- In a pint-sized mason jar of your choice, combine cucumbers, dill, and sliced garlic.
- In a small pan, simmer water, vinegar, Besti, peppercorns, salt, and red pepper flakes.
- Stir occasionally for 10 minutes, the remove from heat and cool mixture to room temperature.
- Pour cooled mixture into the mason jar almost all the way, but leave a ½ space inch at the top.
- Cover and shake a few times before placing in refrigerator. Keep refrigerated for at least 24 hours before serving.

INGREDIENTS

 prep time: 15 min   total time: 45 mins   servings: eight

- **3 medium** zucchinis
- **1 cup** Parmesan cheese
- **2** eggs (can use just the **whites** if you prefer)
- **3 tsp** Cajun seasoning
- Salt & pepper **to taste**
- **Optional:** keto friendly breadcrumbs

Zucchini Fries

DIRECTIONS

- Preheat oven to 425°F and line a baking sheet with parchment paper.
- Cut the ends off of the zucchini and discard.
- Slice the zucchini into thin strips - as 'fry-like' as possible.
- Gently pat the slices dry with paper towel or cheese cloth.
- In a small bowl, beat eggs and stir in 1 tsp Cajun seasoning.
- In a separate bowl, mix together to Parmesan cheese, breadcrumbs (if applicable) and remaining Cajun seasoning.
- Dip the zucchini strips in the egg mixture and coat every piece with Parmesan mixture.
- Arrange the zucchini slices evenly on a baking sheet in a single layer.
- Bake for about 15 minutes, flip, and cook for an additional 15 minutes.
- Enjoy these alone or with your favorite K2 friendly dip!

INGREDIENTS

 prep time: 15 min
 total time: 25 mins
 servings: five

- **2** large ripe (but firm) avocados
- **Juice** from one lemon
- **1** large egg
- **1 cup** super fine blanched almond flour
- **1 cup** grated parmesan cheese
- **Cooking oil spray** of choice

Avocado Fries

DIRECTIONS

- **Baking**: preheat the oven to 400°F. Line a baking sheet with parchment paper and set aside.
- **Air frying**: 375°F. Whisk egg in a small bowl, set aside.
- Slice avocados into thick wedge slices, place in a bowl, squeeze lemon juice on top and gently stir until evenly coated.
- Add almond flour and cheese to food processor and pulse until evenly mixed.
- Lay a piece of parchment paper, down on your countertop, and scoop a tsp of breading mixture onto it.
- Dip one slice in the egg wash, gently shake off any excess egg drippings back into the egg bowl.)
- Try to avoid having any egg drippings in the breading mixture; the moisture causes the breading to clump, making it harder to stick.)

Continued on next page.

CONTINUED

- Place the avocado slice onto the small mound of breading, applying a little pressure so the breading sticks to the bottom of the avocado.
- Sprinkle breading over the surface of the avocado, until it is coated in crumbs.
- Use your fingers to gently press the breading onto the avocado so it sticks and is thoroughly coated. This works better than rolling the avocado in the breading.
- Carefully transfer the slice onto your prepared baking sheet if baking, air fryer basket if air frying.
- Repeat with remaining avocado slices, ensuring they do not overlap or touch. Spray surface of avocado fries with cooking oil spray.
- **Oven**: bake in preheated oven until coating is crispy, about 25 minutes.
- **Air Fryer**: set temperature of air fryer to 375°F, cook for about 10 minutes or until coating is dark golden brown and crispy - and serve while still crispy!
- **Optional**: you can cut some of the bitterness that occurs when the avocado is cooked, by coating the avocados in lemon juice once more after cooking.

INGREDIENTS

 prep time: 10 min  total time: 10 mins   servings: two

- **1 can (4-oz) t**una in spring water, drained (100 g/ 3.5 oz)
- **½ small** red onion, finely diced
- **3 tbsp** mayonnaise - (K2 mayo recipe on **page 138**)
- **½ tsp** Dijon or yellow mustard
- **1 large** cucumber, peeled & seeds removed (240 g/ 8.5 oz)
- **1 medium** spring onion, sliced (15 g/ 0.5 oz) or 1 **bundle** of fresh chives
- Sea salt and pepper **to taste**

Creamy Tuna Cucumber Boats

DIRECTIONS

- To prepare the filling, drain the tuna, and finely dice the red onions
- Mix the drained tuna, red onion, mayonnaise, and mustard in a bowl until combined.
- Season with salt and pepper to taste and set aside.
- Peel the cucumber and cut it in half widthwise and lengthwise to get a total of 4 pieces.
- Use a small spoon (or similar) to scoop the seeds out
- Top the halves with the creamy tuna and fresh spring onions (can sub chives).
- Best served immediately but can be sealed and stored for up to 3 days in the fridge.

INGREDIENTS

 prep time: 10 min  total time: 35 mins   4 yield: 4 slices

- **3 cups** shredded Monterey Jack
- **3 cups** shredded cheddar
- **4 cups** shredded chicken
- 1 avocado, thinly sliced
- **1 tbsp** extra-virgin olive oil
- 1 bell pepper, sliced
- ½ yellow onion, sliced
- **½ tsp** chili powder
- Salt, **to taste**
- **freshly ground black pepper**
- 1 green onion, thinly sliced
- **Dollop** of sour cream, for serving

Cheesy Chicken Quesadillas

DIRECTIONS

- Preheat the oven to 400º and line two baking sheets with parchment paper.
- Heat the oil, sliced bell pepper and onion on a skillet over medium-high heat.
- Stir for 2-3 minutes or until fragrant.
- Add the shredded chicken and spices, stirring for 3 to 5 minutes.
- Transfer to a plate.

Continued on next page ➡

CONTINUED

Cheese "tortillas":
- Mix all of the cheese together in a bowl. Add 1 ½ cups of cheese into the center of both baking sheets. Shape into a circle, mimicking the size of a flour tortilla.
-
- Bake on center rack until just melted and slightly golden around the edge, about 7 to 10 minutes.
- Add onion-pepper mixture, shredded chicken, and avocado slices to one half of each cheese tortilla.
- Let cool slightly, then use the parchment paper and a small spatula to gently lift and fold one side of the "tortilla" over the side with the fillings.
- Return to oven to heat, 3 to 4 minutes more. Repeat to make 2 more quesadillas.
- Garnish with green onion and sour cream before serving.

INGREDIENTS

 prep time: 10 min  total time: 20 mins   12 yield: 12 sticks

Cheese Sticks
- **8 oz.** Havarti
- **3** egg whites
- **½ cup** pork rinds crushed
- **¼ cup** almond flour
- **¼ cup** grated Parmesan
- **1 ½ cup** coconut oil (or enough to fill a medium skillet to about an inch high)

Dipping Sauce
- **2 tbsp** mayonnaise
- **2 tbsp** sour cream
- **1 tsp** apple cider vinegar
- **2 tbsp** chopped dill
- **2 dashes** sriracha, tabasco, or preferred hot sauce
- **¼ tsp** coconut aminos

Cheese Sticks

DIRECTIONS

- Heat the oil to 375°F in a skillet for deep frying.
- Whisk the egg whites in a small, shallow dish
- In a separate shallow dish, combine almond flour, crushed pork rinds, and Parmesan.
- Cut Havarti into ½-inch thick strips

Continued on next page.

- Dredge one of the cheese strips in egg whites, then into the flour mixture, back into the egg whites, and once again back into the flour mixture.
- Repeat with all cheese sticks.
- Carefully place the coated cheese sticks one at a time into the hot oil. Only fry a few at a time so you don't overcrowd the skillet.
- Fry for about 1-3 minutes until they are golden brown, flipping them halfway.
- Transfer to a plate or baking sheet, and cool before serving.
- Combine all dipping sauce ingredients in a small bowl, and enjoy!

INGREDIENTS

 prep time: 20 min   total time: 30 mins   servings: six

- **1 large** sweet onion
- **1 cup** almond flour
- **1 cup** grated Parmesan cheese
- **2 large** eggs
- **1 tbsp** baking powder
- **1 tsp** smoked paprika
- **Salt** and **pepper**
- **1 tbsp** heavy cream
- Cooking spray

Onion Rings

DIRECTIONS

- Cut onion into rings of any desired shape/size.
- In a medium bowl, combine the almond flour, Parmesan cheese, baking powder, smoked paprika, salt, and pepper.
- In a separate bowl, beat eggs and pour in the heavy cream.
- Pat each onion ring dry with a bit of paper towel before dipping it into the egg mixture, fully coating it.
- Remove and gently shake off any excess liquid, then dredge in the almond flour mixture.
- Press the flour mixture into the onions until thoroughly coated.
- Transfer to a parchment lined baking sheet and repeat with the remaining onion.

Continued on next page.

CONTINUED

Air Frying
- Preheat air fryer to 350°F.
- Arrange onions in a single layer, cooking in batches (don't overcrowd)
- Spray rings with cooking spray and fry for 5 minutes.
- Using a spatula or tongs, carefully flip each ring, spray again, and cook for 5 more minutes.

Baking
- Preheat oven to 400°F. Line a baking sheet with parchment paper.
- Arrange the onions in a single layer and spray with cooking spray.
- Bake for 10 minutes, carefully flip, spray with oil once more.
- Bake for an additional 10 to 12 minutes, until crispy and golden.

INGREDIENTS

 prep time: 15 min  total time: 30 mins    servings: eight

- **1 bag** almond flour tortillas (or low carb alternative)
- Avocado oil
- Course sea salt
- Optional: your favorite spices/seasoning

Chips - 4 Ways!

DIRECTIONS - 4 OPTIONS

- Cut the tortillas into desired chip shape.

Frying
- Pour ½ inch of oil over medium-high heat in a large skillet.
- Cook in batches, turning once, until golden brown (about 1 minute per side)
- Remove and place on a plate or tray lined with paper towels.
- Sprinkle immediately with salt, and let cool before serving.

Deep Frying
- Heat the oil to 350° F.
- Cook for about 2 to 2 ½ minutes.
- Remove to a plate lined with paper towels and sprinkle immediately with salt.
- Cool before serving.

Continued on next page.

CHIPS - 4 WAYS, CONTINUED

Baking
- Preheat the oven to 350° F.
- Line a baking sheet with parchment paper and place the tortilla pieces on the baking sheet.
- Brush with oil and sprinkle with salt. Bake for about 20 minutes, flipping once, until golden brown.
- Cool on a wire rack before serving

Air Frying
- Heat air fryer to 325° F.
- Brush or spray the tortillas with oil and sprinkle with salt.
- Cook for 7 minutes. Flip, and cook for 7 minutes longer, until golden brown.
- Cool on a wire rack.

INGREDIENTS

prep time: 15 min
total time: 1 hr 15 mins
servings: six

- **1 ½ lbs** ground beef
- **1 cup** mozzarella cheese cubed (plus optional: grated or sliced topping)
- **¾ cup** cauliflower rice fresh or frozen
- **6** bell peppers medium, green, red, or yellow
- **½** onion medium, diced
- **2 cloves** garlic minced or crushed
- **1 tbsp** tomato paste
- **1 tsp** Italian seasoning, salt and pepper, **to taste**
- **¾ cup** water

Stuffed Bell Peppers

DIRECTIONS

- **Prepare the peppers**: Slice and discard the stemmed tops from each bell pepper. For smaller portions, halve the peppers lengthwise. Use a spoon to scoop and hollow the bell peppers.
- Pre-cook peppers as desired (microwave for 5-6 minutes in a container with ½-inch of water. for the quickest option). To bake, place cut-side down in a casserole dish with the bottom covered in water and top with foil for 20 minutes at 425°F.

Continued on next page.

STUFFED PEPPERS, CONTINUED

Prepare the filling:
- If baking, preheat the oven to 425°F. Heat the grill if grilling.
- Brown ground beef in a skillet over medium heat and break it down into smaller pieces as it cooks. Discard the excess fat and moisture that cooks off.
- Add onion to the pan and cook until soft. Stir in garlic for 1-2 minutes, until fragrant
- Add tomato paste, Italian seasoning, peppers, salt, and water to the pan and mix well. Bring the mixture to a boil, then drop to a simmer until water cooks off. Remove the pan from heat to allow the mixture to cool.
- Stir in cauliflower rice. Once cooled, add in cheese cubes and mix well.
- Fill the bell pepper shells with the meat and cheese mixture, about ¼ cup each. Place the peppers cut side up in a casserole dish for baking or cast-iron pan for grilling.
- Cover casserole dish in foil and place in preheated oven. Bake for 30 to 40 minutes at 425°F, or until the peppers are tender enough to pierce with a fork.
- If **grilling**, place the cast-iron pan on the grill over indirect heat and cook for 30-40 minutes.

KETO 2.0

APPROVED

Soup & Salad Recipes

INGREDIENTS

 prep time: 5 min  total time: 15 mins  2-4 servings: two-four

- **32 oz** broth of choice (4 cups)
- **1 tbsp** soy sauce (can use tamari or coconut aminos as substitute)
- **2 large** eggs
- **3 tsp** grated fresh ginger
- **½ tsp** sesame oil
- **½** garlic salt
- **2** green onions
- Salt, pepper **&** red pepper flakes **to taste**

Egg Drop Soup

DIRECTIONS

- In a medium pot, add broth, soy sauce (tamari or coconut aminos substitute), ginger, sesame oil, and garlic salt. Stir on medium-high heat.
- Once it starts to boil, turn the soup down to a low simmer.
- Gently beat the eggs in small a bowl.
- While stirring the broth mixture at a medium pace, slowly stir in the eggs in one direction to create the egg "ribbons".
- Keep stirring the whole time for best results.
- Add the sliced green onion to the pot and season with salt and pepper, to taste. Divide the soup between 2-4 bowls.
- Looking for more of a bite? Add red pepper flakes for a spicier soup!
- This soup is best served right away, but can be stored for 2-3 days in the fridge.

INGREDIENTS

 prep time: 5 min    total time: 35 mins    6 servings: six

Garlic Butter Lobster:
- **2 tbsp** butter
- **3-4 garlic** cloves
- **1 tbsp** lemon juice
- **16 oz** uncooked Lobster claw meat

Soup Base:
- **1 (32 oz)** carton seafood stock (can sub vegetable stock)
- **1 tbsp** olive oil
- **4** garlic cloves, minced
- **2** carrots, chopped
- **1** small onion, chopped
- **2 stalks** celery, chopped
- **2 tbsp** tomato paste
- **2 tsp** Old Bay (or similar)
- **1 cup** quality dry white wine
- **¾ cup** heavy cream (can sub coconut cream)

Lobster Bisque

DIRECTIONS

- In a large stock pot or Dutch oven heat the olive oil on medium heat.
- Stir in the garlic, onion, carrots and celery and sauté until fragrant.
- Add the vegetable or seafood stock, tomato paste, Old Bay, and white wine. Bring to a light simmer for at least 15 minutes.

Continued on next page.

LOBSTER BISQUE, CONTINUED

- Using a hand/immersion blender, blend the soup until smooth, then slowly stir in the heavy cream.
- Stir once, reduce the heat to low and cover.
- On another skillet, sauté the lobster meat in garlic, butter, and lemon for about 3-5 minutes.
- Add the lobster and garlic butter mixture to the soup.
- Blend again if desired. Let cool before serving.

Chicken, Shrimp & Sausage Gumbo

INGREDIENTS

 **prep time:** 15 min    **total time:** 1 hr 15 mins    **servings:** twelve

- **4** cups any broth, divided
- **1 ½ pound** skinless boneless chicken breast, fat trimmed
- **8 oz** andouille sausage (or similar)
- **1 lb** shrimp, peeled and deveined
- **6** scallions
- **1 cup** onion,
- **1 cup** bell pepper of choice
- **1 (15oz)** can diced tomatoes
- **1 tbsp** extra virgin olive oil
- **3 tbsp** arrowroot powder
- **1** celery stalk
- **1 tsp** dried thyme
- **1 tsp** ground paprika
- **2** bay leaves
- **¼ - 1 tsp** cayenne pepper, to taste
- **3** garlic cloves, minced
- **1 tsp** distilled white vinegar
- **¼ cup** fresh parsley,
- Salt and pepper, **to taste**

Directions on next page.

DIRECTIONS

- Prepare ingredients, slicing vegetables and sausage as desired.
- In a large skillet or Dutch oven, heat olive oil over medium heat until shimmering. Add vegetables, cooking until softened; approximately 5-7 minutes.
- Stir in spices and garlic and cook until fragrant before adding 2 cups of broth and the diced tomatoes.
- Add the chicken to skillet in a single layer.
- Bring to a simmer then cover for about 15-17 minutes. Plate to cool.
- Once cool, use two forks to pull apart the chicken.
- Stir together the remaining broth with the arrowroot powder and add to the pan. Add sausage to the pan and stir to coat everything evenly.
- Bring to a slight boil and simmer for 25 minutes, or until thickened.
- Add pulled chicken and shrimp to the pan and simmer for 10 minutes until shrimp is cooked through.
- Remove bay leaves. Taste and adjust seasonings if desired.
- Stir in scallions and vinegar and serve garnished with parsley.

INGREDIENTS

prep time: 10 min
total time: 30 mins
servings: six

- **1 head** cauliflower, medium
- **1 pound** steamer clams, weighed with shell, then shucked
- **2 cups** chicken broth
- **2 cups** water
- **½** onion, medium
- **6 tbsp** ghee
- **2 tsp** salt
- **1 sprig** rosemary

Clam Chowder

DIRECTIONS

- Scoop 2 tablespoons of the ghee and melt in a large pot. Slice the onions and add to the pot, stirring occasionally, until fragrant and translucent.
- Cut cauliflower into 4 quarters. Shuck the clams.
- Add ¾ of the cauliflower to the pot and set the last ¼ aside.
- Add the chicken broth, water, salt, and remainder of ghee.
- Bring to a boil, reduce to medium heat, cover, and cook for about 10 minutes.
- Roughly chop or break apart the remaining cauliflower.
- Remove the pot from the heat, and very carefully pour into a large blender.

Continued on next page.

CLAM CHOWDER, CONTINUED

- Blend until the mixture is smooth and pour back into the pot.
- Stir in the last of the cauliflower florets, add the clams, and rosemary sprig.
- Bring pot to a simmer and cook for an additional 10-12 minutes.
- Remove rosemary sprig prior to serving and add salt and pepper to taste.
- Optional garnish: dried rosemary and/or crumbled bacon.

INGREDIENTS

 prep time: 10 min  total time: 30 mins **6** servings: six

- **4** cucumbers, chilled
- **½** red onion
- **½ cup** sour cream
- **2 tbsp** fresh dill
- **1 tbsp** mayonnaise
- Salt and pepper **to taste**
- **Optional:** flaky sea salt sprinkled on top

Dill Cucumber Onion Salad

DIRECTIONS

- Cut chilled cucumber and red onion into thin slices.
- Place the chopped veggies in a large mixing bowl.
- In a separate bowl, mix sour cream, mayonnaise, dill, salt, and pepper.
- Pour the dressing on cucumber and onion and mix with a large spoon.
- Toss to thoroughly coat in dressing.
- Transfer to refrigerator to chill for at least 20 minutes.
- When serving, top with salt, additional fresh dill, and pepper.
- Can be great as a salad with your meal, or a refreshing midday snack!

Cobb Salad

 prep time: 10 min  total time: 30 mins   servings: four

INGREDIENTS

RANCH DRESSING
- ½ **cup** mayonnaise
- ¼ **cup** sour cream
- 2 **tsp** lemon juice
- 1 ½ **tsp** dried parsley
- 1 **tsp** dried chives
- 1 tsp dried dill
- ½ **tsp** garlic powder
- ½ **tsp** onion powder
- ½ **tsp** salt
- ¼ - ½ **tsp** black pepper
- 2 - 4 **tbsp** heavy cream (to desired consistency)

COBB SALAD
- 10 slices bacon
- 2 boneless skinless chicken breasts, (trim excess fat)
- 3 hard-boiled eggs
- ½ **tsp** black pepper
- ¼ **tsp** paprika
- 2 **cups** chopped romaine
- 2 avocados, peeled and sliced
- ⅔ **cup** cherry tomatoes, sliced
- ⅓ **cup** sliced green onions
- ⅓ **cup** blue cheese crumbles
- ½ **tsp** salt & pepper (to taste)

Directions on next page.

DIRECTIONS

- Whisk all dressing ingredients (except the heavy cream) in a small mixing bowl.
- Pour in the heavy cream slowly, adding about 1 tbsp at a time, and whisk until desired consistency is reached; set aside.
- In a large skillet, add bacon slices and cook over medium-low heat until crisp.
- When done, place on a plate to cool, and season chicken breasts with salt, pepper and paprika.
- Increase skillet heat to medium high and add chicken breasts,
- Cook 5-6 minutes each side until thoroughly cooked and golden brown. Set aside on a plate.
- Once cooled, slice the chicken and crumble the bacon.
- Create your salad by adding romaine lettuce to large bowl.
- Top with hard-boiled eggs, avocado, tomatoes, green onions, blue cheese, bacon crumbles and sliced chicken.
- Serve drizzled with your delicious homemade ranch dressing!

INGREDIENTS

prep time: 2 mins
total time: 30 mins
servings: six

- 3 ½ **cups** cheddar cheese
- ½ large onion, chopped
- 2 cloves garlic minced
- 3 **cups** chicken broth
- 1 ½ **cups** heavy cream
- 4 **cups** broccoli, finely chopped
- 1 **tbsp** butter
- ½ **tsp** smoked paprika
- 1 **tsp** pepper
- ½ **tsp** salt

Broccoli Cheddar Soup

DIRECTIONS

- In a large pot, add the butter and place it over medium heat.
- Once hot, add the onions and garlic and stir fry for 1-2 minutes, until fragrant.
- Add chicken broth, heavy cream and finely chopped broccoli, smoked paprika, pepper, and salt and bring it to a boil.
- When it just starts to boil, reduce to low and simmer for 20 minutes until the broccoli is tender.
- Add ½ cup of the cheddar cheese and continue adding it in ½ cup increments until combined.
- Remove from the heat and serve (with extra shredded cheese and chopped parsley on top, if desired).

KETO 2.0

APPROVED

Vegan Recipes

INGREDIENTS

 prep time: 5 mins  total time: 20 mins   servings: six

- **1 lb m**ushrooms of choice
- **2 tbsp** olive oil, divided
- **2 tbsp** unsalted butter
- **2 cloves** garlic
- **¼ cup broth** of your choice
- **½ tsp** sea salt, to taste
- **¼ tsp** black pepper, to taste

Sautéed Mushrooms

DIRECTIONS

- Rinse mushrooms in a colander, and pat dry very well. Slice as desired.
- Heat 1 tbsp of olive oil in a large skillet over medium-high heat until simmering.
- Add half of the mushrooms to the pan in a single layer. Sauté for 4-5 minutes, flipping halfway through, until mushrooms are browned and/or liquid evaporates.
- Once slightly browned and reduced in size, push to the sides of the pan.
- Add another tbsp of oil and remaining mushrooms in a single layer in the center of the pan.
- Sauté for 4-5 more minutes, flipping halfway through again, until the second batch is browned, and the liquid has evaporated.
- Season the mushrooms with salt and pepper, to taste, and stir.

Continued on next page.

SAUTÉED MUSHROOMS, CONTINUED

- Reduce heat to medium-low. Push the mushrooms to sides of the pan, make a well and add the butter. Once it melts, add the minced garlic.
- Sauté for about 1 minute, until fragrant. Stir everything in the pan together.
- Sauté for another 1-2 minutes, until the butter absorbs into the mushrooms.
- Add the broth to the pan and use a wooden spoon to scrape the bottom.
- Increase heat to bring to a simmer, and continue to simmer for 2-3 minutes, until the liquid is almost completely absorbed into the mushrooms.

INGREDIENTS

prep time: 20 mins | total time: 25 mins | servings: eight

- **1 head** cauliflower
- **3 eggs** beaten
- **¾ cup** almond flour
- **¾ cup** parmesan cheese, grated
- **1 tsp** garlic powder
- **1 tsp** onion powder
- **½ tsp** salt
- **½ tsp** ground black pepper
- **1 cup** Keto BBQ sauce, divided

Buffalo Cauliflower Wings

DIRECTIONS

- **Air fryer**: preheat to 400°F. Spray the bottom of your air fryer with cooking spray.
- **Oven**: preheat to 425°F. Line a baking sheet with parchment and/or spray with cooking spray.
- Core the cauliflower and cut into large florets.
- Beat the eggs in a small bowl. Add 2 tsp BBQ sauce and stir.
- In a separate bowl, combine the almond flour, Parmesan, garlic powder, onion powder, salt, and pepper.
- Dip the cauliflower florets in the egg, one at a time, and then coat in the almond flour mixture (press firmly with your hands to help the coating stick).
- Add the cauliflower in a single layer, cooking in batches.
- Cook for 5-6 minutes. Flip, respray, and cook for 6 minutes longer.
- Brush with the BBQ sauce and cook for an additional 5 minutes.
- Let cool slightly, serve and enjoy!

INGREDIENTS

prep time: 5 mins | total time: 30 mins | servings: five

- ¼ **cup** sesame oil
- ½ **cup** liquid aminos
- 2 **cloves** garlic, peeled & pressed
- 1 **tbsp** ground ginger
- 2 **tbsp** granulated swerve
- 2 medium eggplants
- chopped green onion or chives for garnish
- Sea salt, **to taste**

Grilled Eggplant

DIRECTIONS

- Cut off eggplant stems and discard.
- Slice eggplant into ⅛ in slices. You should get approximately five slices from each eggplant.
- Combine all but last 2 ingredients into a sauce pan, whisking over medium heat.
- Bring the sauce to a light simmer, stirring often until it begins to thicken.
- Remove sauce from heat and brush onto each slice of eggplant.
- Place on a hot grill.
- Sear each side, brush with more sauce as it caramelizes and sprinkle sea salt to taste.
- Garnish with green onions or chives, and serve with remaining sauce.

INGREDIENTS

prep time: 15 mins
total time: 30 mins
servings: two

- 4 zucchinis (14 **oz**)*
- 1 **tsp** extra virgin olive oil

PESTO SAUCE
- 2 **cups** fresh basil leaves
- ⅓ **cup** sunflower seeds
- ⅓ **cup** extra virgin olive oil
- 3 garlic cloves
- ¼ **tsp** salt, adjust to taste
- ¼ **cup** shredded Parmesan or sub
- ¼ **cup** unsweetened almond milk

Pesto Zucchini Noodles

DIRECTIONS

- Cut off the ends of the zucchini and place in spiralizer. Spiralize half at a time if needed, but try to center the zucchini as best you can and press firmly; the goal is to have long zucchini noodles rather than short, curly ones. Set aside on a plate while you make the pesto. *Can use pre-spiraled zucchini if you don't have a spiralizer.*

- **Pesto Sauce**: Heat a small frying pan under medium heat. Add the sunflower seeds and stir for 2-3 minutes, until fragrant.

- Transfer to a food processor along with all the rest of the pesto ingredients: basil leaves, olive oil, garlic clove, salt, and grated Parmesan.

Continued on next page. ➡

PESTO ZUCCHINI NOODLES, CONTINUED

- Process until a smooth spread forms. Pause to scrape down the sides with a spatula, and process again (if needed) until it forms a consistent spread.
- Heat the olive oil in a large pan on low-medium heat, toss for 2-5 minutes.
- Stir in the homemade sunflower seed pesto and add the unsweetened almond milk, stirring 1-2 minutes until the sauce thickens and forms bubbles on the side of the pan.
- Add more almond milk for a thinner sauce.
- Garnish with additional basil leaves, if desired.
- Best served immediately but can be stored in the fridge for 2-3 days.

KETO 2.0

APPROVED

Vegetable Sides & Dairy Recipes

INGREDIENTS

 prep time: 10 mins  total time: 15 mins    servings: four

- **1** medium head cauliflower (yielding ~ 4 cups cauliflower rice; can sub equivalent amount fresh or frozen cauliflower rice)
- **½ tsp** salt (or ¾ tsp, adjust to taste)
- **⅛ tsp** black pepper (or ¼ tsp, to taste)
- **2 tbsp** olive oil (can use 1 tbsp, but flavor is better with 2)

Cauliflower Rice

DIRECTIONS

- Make cauliflower rice using a grater or by pulsing in a food processor. (Skip to next step if you have ready-made fresh or frozen cauliflower rice.)
- Season the raw cauliflower rice with sea salt and black pepper.
- Heat the olive oil in a large pan or wok over medium-high heat, for 1-2 minutes before adding the cauliflower rice.
- Stir fry for 3-5 minutes, uncovered and stirring occasionally, until cauliflower rice is soft but not mushy (al dente).
- Adjust salt and pepper to taste if desired.
- **Note**: you can add butter and/or any of your preferred seasonings, if desired.
- Store sealed in the fridge for 3-4 days.

INGREDIENTS

 prep time: 10 mins  total time: 20 mins  servings: four

- **1 head** cauliflower riced/grated
- **2** celery stalks
- **2** eggs
- **2 tbsp** coconut aminos or gluten-free soy sauce
- **1 tbsp** sesame oil (or cooking oil of choice)
- ¼ yellow onion diced
- ¼ bell pepper red or yellow, chopped
- **2** green onion stalks
- **1 tbsp** water
- **Salt** and **pepper to taste**

Cauliflower Fried Rice

DIRECTIONS

- Heat half of the sesame oil (or oil of choice) in a large frying pan or wok over medium heat. Add onion, stirring occasionally until fragrant and golden.
- Chop celery and add to pan with cauliflower rice and peppers Cook for 5 to 8 minutes.
- Pour aminos over top of vegetable mixture. Toss to thoroughly coat, stirring quickly.
- Heat remaining sesame oil in small pan on medium-low heat.

Continued on next page.

CAULIFLOWER FRIED RICE, CONTINUED

- Whisk together the eggs, water, salt, and pepper. Pour egg mixture into small pan and scramble.
- Add eggs to the vegetable mixture and mix thoroughly.
- Remove from heat. Add salt and pepper to taste and garnish with green onions.
- Whisk all dressing ingredients (except heavy cream) in a small mixing bowl. Then add heavy cream, starting with 2 tbsp and increasing 1 tbsp at a time, to desired consistency. Set aside.
- To a large skillet, add bacon slices and cook over medium-low heat until crisp. Remove to a plate to cool. Season chicken breasts with salt, pepper and paprika.
- Increase skillet to medium or medium-high heat, and add chicken breasts, cooking 5-6 minutes per side. Set side with chicken, crumble/slice once cooled.
- Assemble salad by adding romaine lettuce to large bowl. Top with hard-boiled eggs, avocado, tomatoes, green onions, blue cheese, bacon crumbles and sliced chicken.
- Serve drizzled with ranch dressing. (Ranch recipe on **page 143**).

INGREDIENTS

 prep time: 5 mins    total time: 15 mins    servings: four

- **1** large head cauliflower (6 cups florets, cut off most of the stems)
- **1 tsp** olive oil
- **2 cloves** garlic, minced
- **½** onion, diced
- **2 tbsp** unsalted butter
- **2 tbsp** cream cheese
- **¾ tsp** salt
- **Chives**

Mashed Cauliflower

DIRECTIONS

- Cut butter and cream cheese into ½ inch chunks. Set aside.
- Wash and roughly break apart or cut cauliflower. Boil or steam cauliflower until tender to pierce with a fork.
- Heat olive oil in a small skillet over medium heat. Add the minced garlic and onion and sauté for about a minute, until fragrant.
- Place the cooked cauliflower, sauteed garlic, butter, cream cheese, and salt into a food processor.
- Purée for 1-2 minutes, until smooth.
- Adjust salt to taste.
- Garnish with chives if desired. You can drizzle some melted butter and/or sprinkle some grated cheese on top if you'd like!
- Best served immediately but can be great for meal prepping. Keep sealed tight in the fridge for 3-4 days.

INGREDIENTS

- **1 lb** asparagus
- **1 tbsp** olive oil
- **1 tsp** garlic powder
- **½ tsp** chipotle salt
- **¼ tsp** fresh ground black pepper
- **1 tbsp** fresh lemon juice
- **½ cup** grated Parmesan cheese
- **¼ tsp** red pepper flakes

 prep time: 5 mins  total time: 25 mins   4   servings: four

Spicy Asparagus

DIRECTIONS

- Preheat air fryer to 390°F or oven to 420°F.
- Trim the ends of your asparagus off. If using thick asparagus, you can slice each one in half.
- Place the asparagus in a bowl.
- Whisk together olive oil, garlic powder, chipotle salt, and black pepper.
- Pour over the asparagus and toss to coat, mixing well.
- If baking, line a baking sheet with parchment paper and spread asparagus in a single layer.
- Spread the same way in air fryer tray, if air frying.
- Cook for 6 minutes for crisp-tender asparagus, or for 10 to 13 minutes for asparagus that is crisp and brown but still tender inside.
- Squeeze fresh lemon juice over the asparagus and sprinkle with Parmesan cheese and red pepper flakes, if desired.

INGREDIENTS

prep time: 5-10 mins
total time: 15 mins
servings: two

- 2 baby Bok choy
- 2 **cloves** of garlic
- 2 **tsp** olive oil
- 2 **tsp** soy sauce (can substitute sriracha, Cholula Hot Sauce, etc.)
- ¼ **tsp** sesame seeds
- ¼ **tsp** red pepper flakes
- 2 **tsp** minced ginger

Garlic Roasted Bok Choy

DIRECTIONS

- Preheat the oven to 425°F.
- Wash the baby Bok choy thoroughly and slice in half lengthwise.
- Pat dry with paper towel.
- Peel and smash 2 garlic cloves. This will help ensure they do not burn in the oven.
- Place a medium oven-proof pan over medium-high heat.
- Add 2 tsp of olive oil, garlic and ginger, sautéing until fragrant.
- Add the baby Bok choy to the pan, cut sides down.
- Drizzle 2 tsp of soy (or hot) sauce on top, and place in the oven for 7-10 minutes.
- The Bok choy should be cooked through, but still crunchy.
- Transfer to a plate and garnish with sesame seeds and red pepper flakes, to taste.

INGREDIENTS

 prep time: 5 mins  total time: 35 mins  2-4 servings: two-four

- **1 bag/package** Brussels sprouts
- **4 tbsp** minced garlic
- **1 tbsp** sriracha sauce (can sub alternative K2 friendly hot sauce)
- **3 tbsp** soy sauce (can sub tamari or coconut aminos)
- Drizzle of olive oil
- Salt and pepper, **to taste**

Sriracha Brussels Sprouts

DIRECTIONS

- Preheat the oven to 400°F.
- While preheating, wash the Brussels sprouts and cut in half. Remove any hard pieces.
- Toss them in olive oil with salt, pepper, and garlic. Ensure the sprouts are evenly coated.
- Roast for 20-25 minutes or until crispy.
- In a small bowl, mix soy sauce and Sriracha sauce to taste.
- When sprouts are done, toss them in the sauce.

INGREDIENTS

- **2 ½ cups** filtered water
- **1 ½ tsp** salt, divided
- **15 oz** raw jicama
- **1 tbsp + 2 tsp** avocado oil
- **½ tsp** ground turmeric
- **¼ tsp** garlic powder
- **¼ tsp** paprika
- **⅛ tsp** onion powder
- **2 tsp** fresh parsley

prep time: 15 mins
total time: 45 mins
servings: six (6)

Jicama Fries

DIRECTIONS

- Preheat the oven to 400°F and line baking sheet with foil.
- Using a vegetable peeler, peel skin from jicama.
- Slice the peeled jicama into desired fry shape and size.
- Using a medium pot set on high heat, add water and ½ tsp salt.
- Bring to a boil.
- Add sliced jicama, cover pot, and boil for 10 minutes. Remove pot from heat and drain water.
- Transfer jicama to a large mixing bowl, drizzle with avocado oil and add remaining salt, turmeric, garlic powder, paprika, and onion powder. Toss fries using tongs until fully coated in oil and spices.
- Transfer onto the prepared baking sheet in single layer.
- Bake for 20 minutes, flip, and bake for an additional 20 minutes.
- Remove from oven and allow to cool slightly before garnishing with finely chopped fresh parsley and/or your favorite K2 friendly dip.

INGREDIENTS

prep time: 5 mins
total time: 45 mins
servings: six

- **1** medium spaghetti squash
- **4 tsp** avocado oil
- **¼ tsp** salt
- **¼ tsp** pepper
- **¼ tsp** red pepper flakes
- **4** pieces of bacon
- **2** green onion stems
- Optional: K2 friendly pasta sauce

Spaghetti Squash with Bacon

DIRECTIONS

- Preheat the oven to 425°F.
- Line a baking sheet with parchment paper and lightly grease with oil or cooking spray.
- Using a sharp knife, slice the spaghetti squash in half.
- Scoop out the seeds and drizzle lightly with avocado oil. Add salt and pepper and use a fork to poke holes all over the squash.
- Place the spaghetti squash halves onto the lined baking sheet with the cut side down.
- Roast in the oven for 25-35 minutes until the skin pierces easily with a fork or knife. Remove and let the squash rest on the pan for 10 minutes.
- When cool to the touch, use a fork to scrape the strands from the sides of the squash. Sprinkle crumbled bacon, chopped green onions, and red pepper flakes on top before serving.
- **Optional**: add your favorite K2 friendly pasta sauce!

INGREDIENTS

prep time: 20 mins | total time: 40 mins | servings: eight

- 1 cabbage
- 6 slices bacon
- 3 tbsp bacon grease
- ½ small onion
- ½ cup chicken broth
- ½ tsp salt
- ¼ tsp garlic powder
- ¼ tsp pepper
- ¼ tsp paprika

Fried Cabbage with Bacon

DIRECTIONS

- Fry bacon to desired crispiness. Remove bacon from the pan and set aside on a paper towel. Reserve 3 tbsp of bacon grease in the pan.
- Chop onion and cabbage in small bite-sized pieces.
- Sauté onion in the bacon grease until fragrant and soft.
- Add the cabbage, chicken broth, garlic powder, salt, pepper, and paprika to the skillet and bring it to a boil. Once boiling, cover with a lid and reduce heat to medium-low.
- Simmer cabbage for 20 minutes or until it reaches desired tenderness.
- Once done, remove from pan to rest for a few minutes.
- Crumble the cooked bacon, sprinkle on top and serve.

KETO 2.0
APPROVED
Poultry Recipes

INGREDIENTS

prep time: 15 mins
total time: 15 mins
servings: four

- **1 lbs** shredded cooked chicken
- **½ cup** mayonnaise
- **⅓** cup celery, diced
- **½** green pepper cubed
- **½** red pepper cubed
- **¼** small onion finely chopped
- **2 tbsp** lemon juice
- **1 tsp** Dijon mustard
- Romaine lettuce leaves, for serving
- Salt and pepper **to taste**
- **½ tsp** fresh dill

Chicken Salad Lettuce Wrap

DIRECTIONS

- Finely chop the onion and celery and cube the bell peppers to desired shape.
- Combine chicken and vegetables in a large bowl.
- Add lemon juice and mustard to the mixture. Season with salt, pepper, and dill to taste.
- Arrange the romaine leaves on a serving platter.
- Top each romaine lettuce leaf with ⅓ cup of the chicken salad mixture and serve.

- **Tip**: this is the perfect way to use up any leftover chicken you may have!

INGREDIENTS

prep time: 30 mins | total time: 2 hrs 30 mins | yield: two skewers

- **4** chicken breasts (2 lbs)
- **⅓ cup** extra virgin olive oil
- **6 tbsp** herbs of choice (mint, parsley, oregano, dill, etc.)
- **1** lemon, juiced
- **1 tsp** salt
- **½ tsp** black pepper
- Wood or metal skewers

Chicken Souvlaki Skewers

DIRECTIONS

- To start your chicken marinade, cut meat into 2-inch pieces and place in a bowl. Add olive oil, chopped herbs, juice from 1 lemon, salt and pepper.
- Mix until evenly coated. Cover and refrigerate for at least 2 hours or overnight.
- Once ready to cook, pierce 4 to 5 pieces onto each skewer.
- Cook the skewers in batches on a hot a griddle pan undisturbed for 3 to 4 minutes, and then turn 90 °F, until browned and cooked though on all sides.
- Brush each skewer with the leftover marinade when flipping.
- *It takes approximately 12 to 16 minutes for each skewer to fully cook.
- Remove from the pan and set aside to cool for 5 minutes before serving.
- Serve with any salads, sides or dips. K2 friendly tzatziki is an excellent choice!

INGREDIENTS

 prep time: 5 mins   total time: 20 mins  servings: four

- **4** thin sliced chicken breasts
- **½ cup** oil-packed sun-dried tomatoes
- **2** cloves garlic, minced
- **1 cup** chopped spinach
- **2 tbsp** butter
- **1 cup** heavy cream
- **1 tsp** paprika
- **1 tsp** garlic powder
- **1 tsp** salt

Creamy Tuscan Chicken

DIRECTIONS

- Massage all spices into the chicken, ensuring to evenly coat it.
- Heat a large, heavy skillet on medium heat. Add the butter to the skillet.
- When the butter has melted add the chicken breasts and cook 5 minutes per side or until cooked through.
- Remove the chicken to a plate and set aside.
- Add the heavy cream, sun-dried tomatoes, and garlic to the pan and stir well to combine.
- Let the sauce cook, stirring often for 2-3 minutes to thicken over low heat.
- Add the spinach and stir well. Continue cooking over low heat until just wilted and sauce has thickened.
- Return the chicken to the skillet and coat thoroughly with the sauce. Serve immediately with desired sides.

INGREDIENTS

prep time: 20 mins | total time: 55 mins | 12 servings: twelve

- **1 cup** heavy cream
- **2 ½ cups** cooked chicken
- **4 oz** grated sharp Cheddar cheese
- **3 cups** chopped, cooked broccoli
- **¼ cup** sliced almonds
- **4 tbsp** butter
- **½ (8 oz)** package cream cheese
- Salt and ground pepper, **to taste**
- **¾ cup** crushed pork rinds or pork rind panko
- **1 tbsp** extra virgin olive oil (or similar)

Chicken and Broccoli Casserole

DIRECTIONS

- Preheat the oven to 350°F. Spread olive oil spread over the bottom and sides of a 9x13-inch baking/casserole dish.
- Cut chicken into cubes and arrange in a single layer in the dish.
- Spread the cooked broccoli evenly on top and sprinkle with almonds.
- Melt the butter in a saucepan over medium heat.
- Slowly pour in cream, stirring for 1 to 2 minutes before adding the cream cheese. Reduce heat and stir until melted and smooth, an additional 2 to 3 minutes.
- Add Cheddar cheese and stir until melted, 2 to 3 minutes.
- Season with salt and pepper. Pour sauce over chicken, broccoli, and almonds, top with crushed pork rinds.
- Bake in the oven for 25 to 30 minutes until top is bubbly.

INGREDIENTS

 prep time: 6 hrs    total time: 6 hrs 50 mins   14   yield: 14 legs

- **4 lbs** (14 count) chicken drumsticks
- **¼ cup** olive oil, (light oil, not extra virgin)
- **4** garlic cloves, pressed or minced
- **4 tbsp** fresh parsley
- **3 tbsp** lemon juice
- **2 tbsp** Dijon mustard
- **½ tsp** chili powder, or similar
- **¼ tsp** ground cumin
- **¼ tsp** sesame seeds
- **Dash** of cinnamon
- Salt and pepper, **to taste**

Marinated Chicken Drumsticks

DIRECTIONS

Marinade:
- Press garlic and chop parsley before adding to a small bowl. Mix in the rest of the marinade ingredients and combine until thoroughly coated.
- Place the drumsticks in a large mixing bowl or Ziploc bag. Pour in the marinade and toss to evenly distribute.
- Cover with plastic wrap or seal the bag and marinate at least 6 hours. If you can, toss the chicken once halfway through marinating.

Continued on next page.

MARINATED CHICKEN DRUMSTICKS, CONTINUED

- When ready to prepare the marinated chicken, preheat the oven to 400°F and line a baking sheet with foil or parchment paper.
- Place the chicken on the tray, skin side down, in a single layer.
- While the oven preheats, brush chicken legs with any extra marinade (optional).
- Bake on the center rack for 20-25 minutes, flip, and bake additional 20-25 minutes skin-side-up.
- Broil on high heat 2 to 3 minutes per side or until skins have browned and crispy.
- Garnish with parsley and sesame seeds and serve.

INGREDIENTS

 prep time: 10 mins   total time: 1 hr   servings: four

- 4 (8 oz) chicken thighs (skin-on and bone-in)
- 1 tsp paprika
- 4 slices bacon
- ⅓ cup low-sodium broth
- 4 oz sliced mushrooms
- ¼ cup heavy whipping cream
- 2 green onions
- Salt and pepper, to taste

Chicken Thighs

DIRECTIONS

- Preheat the oven to 400°F.
- Season all sides of the chicken thighs with spices. Slice green onion and separate green pieces from white. Set aside.
- Cut bacon into ½ inch pieces and cook in an oven-safe pan or cast-iron skillet over medium-high heat for a few minutes, until browned. Remove from skillet and place on a paper towel-lined plate. Pat the excess grease dry in the skillet.
- Return skillet to medium heat and cook chicken thighs for 3 to 4 minutes. Flip chicken and place the oven-safe skillet in the oven.
- Bake for approximately 30 minutes, or until the internal temperature reaches 165°F. Remove chicken to a plate and cover.
- Reserve 2 tbsp of drippings from the skillet.

Continued on next page.

CHICKEN THIGHS, CONTINUED

- Return skillet to the stove over medium-high heat.
- Pour in broth and mushrooms, cook about 3 to 4 minutes until soft.
- Pour in heavy whipping cream and whisk together until it starts to simmer, then reduce heat to medium-low.
- Return chicken and any juices back into skillet.
- Top with bacon and green onions.
- Spoon sauce over the chicken when serving.

INGREDIENTS

prep time: 10 mins
total time: 20 mins
servings: six (6)

- **3 large** boneless, skinless chicken breasts
- **½ cup** almond flour
- **¼ cup** grated Parmesan cheese
- **1 tsp** Italian seasoning
- **½ tsp** salt
- **½ tsp** pepper
- **4 tbsp** butter (not all at once)
- **2 tbsps** olive oil
- **2 tbsps** olive oil
- **½ cup** dry white wine
- **¼ cup** freshly squeezed lemon juice
- **2 tbsp** capers
- **2 tbsp** heavy cream (more if desired)

Chicken Piccata

DIRECTIONS

- Slice the thick chicken breast as if you are going to 'butterfly' them, but instead cut all the way through.
- Place plastic wrap over the chicken and pound until thin.
- In a bowl combine the almond flour, parmesan and herbs.
- Dredge the thin chicken breast in the mixture and make sure it is coated well on both sides. Let the breaded chicken sit in the fridge 10 minutes to make sure the coating adheres well.
- Heat 1 tbsp of the butter and all of the olive oil in the skillet.

Continued on next page.

CHICKEN PICCATA, CONTINUED

- Sear the chicken about 3 minutes on each side, until golden brown.
- Transfer the browned chicken onto a plate.
- In the same pan add the wine, scraping the pan to deglaze it. Add the lemon juice, capers, heavy cream and remaining butter to the skillet and stir.
- When the sauce has reduced slightly, add the chicken back to the skillet. and cook 2-3 minutes.
- Top with lemon wedges, parmesan and parsley if desired.

INGREDIENTS

prep time: 15 mins | total time: 30 mins | yield: 30 nuggets

- **12.5 oz** canned chicken
- **1 cup** shredded mozzarella cheese
- **1 large** egg
- **½ cup** ground sunflower seed meal
- **½ tsp** garlic powder
- **¼ tsp** onion powder
- **½ cup** crushed pork rinds
- **⅛ tsp** ground cayenne pepper
- Salt and pepper, **to taste**

Chicken Nuggets

DIRECTIONS

- Preheat the oven to 450°F. Line baking sheet with parchment paper and coat the parchment in cooking oil/spray of choice. Drain the canned chicken.
- In a medium bowl, combine canned chicken, shredded mozzarella, ground sunflower seed meal, egg, garlic powder, onion powder, and pepper. Whether by hand or electric mixer, mix until thoroughly combined.
- In a smaller bowl, mix crushed pork rinds and cayenne pepper.
- Spoon out chicken mixture 2 tbsp at a time, forming each mound into your desired nugget shape.

Continued on next page.

CHICKEN NUGGETS, CONTINUED

- Coat all sides of the nuggets in the seasoned pork rinds before placing on the lined baking sheet. Do not discard leftover pork rinds.
- Transfer to oven and bake for 6-8 minutes.
- Remove from oven and flip each nugget.
- Sprinkle remaining crushed pork rinds onto the other side of nuggets before returning to the oven.
- Bake for additional 6-8 minutes.
- Allow nuggets time to cool slightly before serving on their own or with your favorite K2 friendly sauce.

INGREDIENTS

 prep time: 15 mins  total time: 35 mins  servings: eight

- **2 lbs** chicken wings
- **⅔ cup** K2 friendly hot (or BBQ) sauce
- **½ cup** melted butter
- **2 tbsp** white vinegar
- **¼ tsp** Worcestershire sauce
- **¼ tsp** cayenne pepper
- **¼ tsp** garlic powder
- **¼ tsp** salt
- **¼ tsp** red pepper flakes
- **Dash** of baking powder
- **4** celery stalks, for serving

Baked Chicken Wings

DIRECTIONS

- Pre-heat your oven to 400°F.
- Dry the chicken and season with salt, garlic powder, red pepper flakes, and baking powder.
- Arrange the chicken wings on a lined tray and place in the oven when ready.
- While the wings are in the oven, melt the butter in a large bowl, and combine the hot (or BBQ) sauce, vinegar, and Worcestershire.
- Cut the celery stalks in 3-inch pieces and set aside.
- Cook the wings for 10 minutes, flip, and cook an additional 10 minutes. Internal temperature should reach 165 °F
- Once the wings have cooked through, baste with the sauce from the tray.
- Serve with celery or desired K2 friendly side.

INGREDIENTS

prep time: 5 mins
total time: 20 mins
servings: two

- **2 5-oz** duck breasts
- **2 tsp** liquid honey
- **½ tsp** Chinese 5-spice
- **¼ tsp** sesame seeds
- **2 tbsp** K2 soy sauce (can sub coconut aminos)
- **1 tsp** coconut oil
- Diced chives, sprouts or green onions to **garnish**

Honey Soy Duck Breast

DIRECTIONS

- Preheat the oven to 180°F.
- Rub the Chinese 5-spice into the duck breasts, coating evenly.
- On medium heat, fry the duck breasts skin-side-down in the coconut oil over until crispy and golden.
- Flip to cook the sides and bottom for an additional 3-4 minutes, or until the meat is no longer pink.
- Transfer to an oven-safe dish and cook on a middle rack in the oven for 12 to 15 minutes.
- Remove to a plate, cover lightly and rest for 10 minutes before slicing into bite-sized pieces. Reserve pan for next step.
- Add the soy sauce, honey to the pan, simmering with juices from the sliced duck. Simmer until the sauce has slightly thickened and starts to bubble.
- Plate the duck with your choice of sides, spooning the sauce over the top before serving. Top with sesame seeds, if desired.

KETO 2.0

APPROVED

Beef & Lamb Recipes

INGREDIENTS

 prep time: 10 mins  total time: 1 hr 10 mins  servings: six

- 1 ½ **lbs** ground beef
- 2 **cups** beef broth
- 15 **oz** canned diced tomatoes
- 1 yellow onion, diced
- 1 green pepper, diced
- 1 jalapeno, minced
- 1 **clove** garlic, minced
- ¼ **cup** tomato paste
- 2 **tbsp** chili powder
- 1 **tsp** cumin
- Salt and pepper, **to taste**

Chili

DIRECTIONS

- Start by adding the ground beef, onion, and bell pepper to a large deep pot and cook over medium heat, breaking up the meat as it cooks.
- Once the meat is cooked through, drain the fat from pan.
- Add the jalapeno, garlic, tomato paste, diced tomatoes, beef broth, chili powder, cumin, and salt and stir. (Feel free to adjust with desired alternative ingredients)
- Bring to a boil and reduce to a simmer. Simmer for at least 20 minutes (the longer the better) for best taste and texture.
- Serve with sour cream and shredded cheddar, or however desired.
- **Tip**: If the chili isn't too runny, you can serve on lettuce boats as 'Sloppy Joes'!

INGREDIENTS

 prep time: 20 mins
 total time: 1 hr 50 mins
 servings: eight

- **9** corn husks

Masa Harina:
- **2 ½ cups** super fine almond flour
- **½ cup** ground flaxseed meal
- **1 cup** butter or lard
- **½ cup** water
- **1 tsp** salt

Beef Filling
- **1 tbsp** extra virgin olive oil
- **½ pound** ground beef
- **2 oz** shredded cheddar cheese
- **½ tbsp** chili powder
- **⅛ tsp** dried oregano
- **¼ tsp** paprika
- **¾ tsp** ground cumin
- Salt and pepper, **to taste**

Beef Tamales

DIRECTIONS

- Place corn husks in a pot of hot water and use a plate to keep them submerged.
- Cook over medium heat. When it gets close to simmering, lower the heat and leave for 30 minutes. Remove and dry the cornhusks, set aside.
- Heat olive oil on high heat in a large pan. Add ground beef and cook until browned.

Continued on next page.

BEEF TAMALES, CONTINUED

- Mix chili powder, oregano, paprika, cumin and salt in a small bowl. Stir in the ground beef and coat evenly. Divide into 8 portions.
- Microwave water and butter for the Masa Harina. Mix in almond flour, flax seed meal and salt.
- Lay out one of the corn husks. Add ⅛ of the Masa Harina to the corn husk and form into a rectangle along the longest edge.
- Add ⅛ of the ground beef in the middle, and sprinkle ⅛ of the cheese on top.
- Bring the edges of the corn husk together and roll the corn husk around itself. Fold it in the middle, leaving the long end open.
- Cut one of the cornhusks into thin strips to tie together the tamales.
- Repeat with the remaining 7 corn husks, cover in a steam basket, for 1 hour.
- Allow to cool enough to handle before unwrapping the corn husks.
- Best served with salsa verde or chili sauce.

INGREDIENTS

 prep time: 5 mins    total time: 3 hrs 30 mins    servings: six

- **1 lb** flank steak (thinly sliced)
- **¼ cup** coconut aminos (or soy sauce)
- **½ tbsp** Worcestershire sauce (optional, for flavor)
- **1 tsp** garlic powder
- **1 tsp** onion powder
- **1 tbsp** Besti Brown Monk Fruit Allulose Blend
- **½ tsp** crushed red pepper flakes
- Salt and pepper, **to taste**

Beef Jerky

DIRECTIONS

- Slice beef thinly, against the grain and place in a large mixing bowl.
- Add aminos, Worcestershire sauce (if using), all the spices, and the Monk fruit blend to the bowl.
- Mix well before refrigerating for at least 30 minutes or overnight, up to 24 hours.
- Preheat the oven to 175°F. Line a large baking sheet with foil and place an oven-safe non-stick cooling rack on top.
- Arranged the beef strips in a single layer on the wire rack, taking care not to overcrowd.
- Bake keto beef jerky for 3-4 hours, flipping the beef halfway through. Jerky should be dry and firm but still pliable. Cool completely.
- Seal in an air-tight container and store in a cool, dark place for 1-2 months (or frozen for up to a year! Just thaw before serving).

INGREDIENTS

prep time: 10 mins • total time: 1 hr 45 mins • servings: ten

- **4 cups** beef broth
- **2-3 lbs** corned beef brisket
- **1** cabbage
- **1** onion, peeled and quartered
- **4** garlic cloves
- **1 bulb** fresh ginger, peeled and sliced

(**Optional**) Homemade Pickling Spice:
- **1 tsp** yellow mustard seeds
- **1 tsp** whole black pepper corns
- **1 tsp** coriander seeds
- **½ tsp** allspice
- **3** whole cloves (or 1/4 tsp ground)
- **3** bay leaves

Instant Pot Corned Beef Cabbage

DIRECTIONS

- Rinse and dry the brisket and place in the Instant Pot on the rack.
- Add all ingredients but cabbage. Cook on high for 80-90 minutes.
- Allow the steam to release naturally for about 10 minutes before remove beef to set aside.
- Remove everything else from the pot and strain the cooking liquid.
- Return 1 ½ cups of the liquid to the pot.
- Cut cabbage into 8 wedges but leave the core in so it holds together.
- Add the cabbage to the pressure cooker and pressure cook on HIGH for 4 minutes, then quickly release the steam.
- Once the corned beef has cooled, cut (against the grain) into ⅛-inch slices. Serve with a cabbage wedge on the side, if desired.

INGREDIENTS

prep time: 20 mins | total time: 2 hrs 30 mins | servings: ten (10)

- **3 lbs** beef brisket
- **16 oz** fresh mushrooms, sliced
- **¼ cup** avocado oil
- **1** white onion, finely chopped
- **2 tsp** minced garlic
- **2 tsp** ground thyme
- **1 ½ cups** beef broth
- **2 tbsp** apple cider vinegar
- **¾ cup** sour cream
- **¼ cup** mayonnaise
- **1 ½ tsp** xanthan gum
- Salt and black pepper, **to taste**

Beef Stroganoff

DIRECTIONS

- Trim the fat off the brisket and chop into ½ inch pieces.
- Place a large saucepan over medium heat, and add avocado oil, onion, and minced garlic. Sauté until onion and garlic are semi-translucent fragrant.
- Add beef, thyme, salt, and pepper and sauté.
- Stir frequently and make sure to brown all sides of beef. Continue until cooked thoroughly, depending on how well-done you'd like the beef to be.
- Reduce the heat to medium-low and pour in the broth and vinegar.

Continued on next page.

BEEF STROGANOFF, CONTINUED

- Simmer uncovered for 30 minutes, stirring occasionally.
- Stir in mushrooms until coated, cover the pan with lid, and simmer for additional 1 hour, 30 minutes. Stir occasionally.
- Remove pan from heat.
- Stir in sour cream and mayonnaise until thoroughly incorporated.
- Stir in xanthan gum, ¼ tsp at a time until liquid thickens.
- Cover with lid and let it sit covered for 10 minutes before serving.
- Optional garnish: fresh thyme and/or black pepper.

INGREDIENTS

 prep time: 5 mins total time: 25 mins  servings: four

- 1 ½ pounds flank steak
- 1 sweet red bell pepper
- 1 medium onion
- 1 tbsp avocado oil
- 2 tsp minced ginger
- 2 tbsp minced garlic
- ½ cup soy sauce (can sub tamari or coconut aminos)
- ½ cup water
- ¾ cup granulated sweetener
- ¼ tsp red pepper flakes
- 3 large green onion stems
- ¼ tsp xanthan gum

Mongolian Beef

DIRECTIONS

- In a large skillet, heat avocado oil over medium-high heat. Add chopped onions and bell peppers, season with salt and pepper, to taste.
- Reduce the heat to medium-low and cook, stirring frequently until the onions are cooked and the peppers are tender and slightly browned. Process takes around 15-20 minutes. While you wait, chop the green onion stems and set aside.
- In a medium saucepan, heat 1 tbsp of avocado oil over medium heat.

Continued on next page.

MONGOLIAN BEEF, CONTINUED

- Add ginger, garlic, and red pepper flakes, stirring for 30 seconds.
- Add the soy sauce, water, and sweetener to a boil and simmer until thickened (approximately 4-5 minutes).
- Put the sauce in a bowl and set aside.
- Slice the steak against the grain into ¼-inch slices with your knife at a 45-degree angle. Try to keep the slices similar sized, cutting any larger pieces in half.
- In a medium-large skillet, heat avocado oil over medium-high heat.
- Add beef to pan in small batches, cooking each side for 2-3 minutes.
- Add the sauce to the pan along with the xanthan gum, peppers and onions, and green onions.
- Stir to coat the meat and vegetables completely.
- Let cool and serve with desired garnish and sides.
- **Tip**: this goes great with cauliflower rice or served on a lettuce boat!

INGREDIENTS

 prep time: 10 mins    total time: 1 hr 15 mins    servings: twelve

- ½ cup blanched Almond Flour
- ½ large onion diced
- 8 cloves garlic minced
- 3 oz tomato paste
- 2 tbsp Worcestershire sauce or coconut aminos
- 2 large eggs
- 1 tbsp Italian seasoning
- 2 tsp salt
- ½ tsp black pepper
- 2 lbs ground beef
- ½ cup ketchup (K2 friendly ketchup recipe, **page 137**).

Meatloaf

DIRECTIONS

- Preheat the oven to 350°F.
- In a large bowl, combine all meat and ketchup (Can sub K2 friendly tomato sauce). Mix well.
- Add in the meat, folding and mixing until fully incorporated. Do not overmix.
- Transfer the mixture into a loaf pan, spreading evenly.
- Bake for 25-30 minutes. Remove from oven, spread ketchup (or tomato sauce) on top of the meatloaf.

Continued on next page.

MEATLOAF, CONTINUED

- Return to the oven and bake for 25-45 minutes more.
- Meatloaf is fully cooked when internal temperature reaches 160°F. Cook time will vary depending on meatloaf thickness.
- Rest for 10 minutes before slicing.
- If possible, use a serrated bread knife when slicing.
- **Tip**: this dish goes great with mashed cauliflower!

INGREDIENTS

prep time: 20 mins total time: 25 mins servings: four

Enchiladas
- **8 oz** deli turkey
- **1 cup** cheese, grated
- **1 lb** ground beef
- **3 oz.** cauliflower, riced
- **¼ cup** red onion
- **1 tbsp** chili powder
- **1 tsp** ground cumin
- **1 tbsp** olive oil
- **½ tsp** onion powder
- **½ tsp** garlic powder
- **¼ tsp** salt
- **½ cup** water

Sauce
- **2 tbsp** chili powder
- **1 tsp** ground cumin
- **15 oz** tomato sauce
- **½ tsp** garlic powder
- Salt and pepper, **to taste**

Beef Enchiladas

DIRECTIONS

- Preheat the oven to 350°F. Grease a baking pan (a 9" x 12" pan works great for 4 servings).
- Combine all sauce ingredients in a bowl. Set aside.
- Pour olive oil in a large pan over medium heat.
- Add ground beef, onion, cauliflower rice, chili powder, cumin, onion powder, garlic powder, salt, and water. Stir well.

Continued on next page.

BEEF ENCHILADAS, CONTINUED

- Cook for about 7 to 10 minutes until beef is cooked through.
- Add half the sauce to the browned beef mixture. Put two slices of turkey together, overlapping each other, to form a long roll.
- Place 4-5 tbsp of beef on the turkey, lengthwise and slightly off-center.
- Tightly roll the beef mixture inside the turkey (repeat, to make two rolls per serving).
- Place beef-stuffed rolls into the baking dish and spread half the cheese evenly across the surface. Pour the remainder of the enchilada sauce on top and sprinkle with the rest of the cheese.
- Bake for 8-10 minutes or until cheese has melted on top.
- If desired, top with sour cream and jalapenos before serving.
- **Tip**: This recipe is just as delicious with ground turkey or chicken!

Optional Toppings
- pickled jalapeños
- **¼ cup** sour cream

INGREDIENTS

prep time: 15 mins
total time: 35 mins
servings: six

- **1 ½ – 2 lbs** flank steak

Chimichurri Sauce
- **2 tbsp** fresh garlic, peeled
- **½ cup** fresh parsley
- **¼ cup** fresh cilantro
- **1 cup** olive oil or avocado oil
- **¼ cup** fresh lemon juice
- **1 tbsp** dried oregano
- **C**rushed red pepper, to taste
- **Salt** and **pepper,** to taste

Chimichurri Flank Steak

DIRECTIONS

Marinating the steak:
- If cutting your steak, be sure to cut against the grain. Place in a large baking dish or plastic bag and add ⅓ cup chimichurri. Coat well and rest for at least 30 minutes.
- Sear the steaks: Heat a large cast iron skillet over medium-high heat for about 3 minutes. Remove steaks from chimichurri and scrape off excess marinade. Pat dry and sprinkle with a modest amount of salt.
- If working with two pieces of steak, pour 1 tbsp of avocado oil into a cast-iron skillet and let heat about 30 seconds or until shimmering but not smoking.

Continued on the next page.

CHIMICHURRI FLANK STEAK, CONTINUED

- Once heated, use a pair of long tongs and carefully place steaks in skillet.
- Cook 3-4 minutes on each side, depending on the thickness.
- For the chimichurri sauce, add the garlic, fresh parsley and cilantro to a blender and pulse until finely chopped.
- Add all remaining chimichurri sauce ingredients and pulse in the blender until well combined. Set aside.
- Remove steak from skillet and let rest on a cutting board for 5 minutes. Repeat with any additional pieces, if applicable.
- After resting, cut the steak into ½ inch slices against the grain.
- Arrange on a large serving platter and top with fresh chimichurri sauce.
- Serve with additional chimichurri, if desired.

INGREDIENTS

prep time: 20 mins
total time: 25 mins
servings: six

- **2 lbs** flank or skirt steak
- **¼ cup** avocado oil
- **2 tbsp** lime juice
- **¼ cup** cilantro minced
- **2** bell pepper sliced
- **¼** medium onion, thinly sliced
- **½ tsp** salt
- **¼ tsp** chili powder
- **¼ tsp** lime zest

Fajitas

DIRECTIONS

- Preheat the oven to 425°F and set aside a large baking pan.
- Cut against the grain of the steak to make strips ¼ inch thick.
- Pour in avocado oil and lime juice, add cilantro, bell peppers, onion and steak into a bag or container and marinate (at room temperature) sealed for at least 10 minutes.
- Use tongs or a fork to remove all desired ingredients from the bag and spread evenly on tray (lightly greased or lined with parchment paper) in a single layer.
- Place a tray in the oven to cook for 10 minutes. Remove from oven and carefully flip the steak and veggies.
- Switch the oven to broil and cook on high heat for an additional 5-7 minutes. Remove fajitas from oven.
- Combine salt, chili powder, and lime zest and sprinkle on top.
- Prepare as desired and serve immediately.

INGREDIENTS

 prep time: 20 mins   total time: 12.5 hrs  servings: twelve

- **6 lbs** pork ribs
- **1 cup** keto barbeque sauce
- **2 cups** wood chips, soaked in a bowl of water
- **2 tbsp** salt
- **1 tsp** smoked paprika
- **½ tsp** onion powder
- **½ tsp** garlic powder
- **½ tsp** ground ginger
- **¼ tsp** black pepper
- Vegetable oil
- Aluminum foil (heavy duty)

BBQ Ribs

DIRECTIONS

- Combine spices in a small bowl and place a sheet of foil on a baking tray, leaving a 2-inch overhang on all sides.
- Pat ribs dry with paper towel and rub the spice mixture until fully coated on all sides.
- Place rib racks (bone side down) on the baking sheet. Cover with another sheet of foil and crimp edges tightly.
- Refrigerate 8 to 24 hours.
- Preheat the oven to 225° F and place covered baking sheet on the center rack, baking for 4 hours.
- Remove from oven, rest for 10 minutes.

Continued on next page.

DIRECTIONS

- Preheat an outdoor grill for medium heat.
- Drain wood chips and place in an aluminum foil packet, poking holes in the packet.
- Place the foil packet on the hottest part of the grill and close the lid.
- Once the chips begin to smoke, oil the grate, remove foil and place ribs on top.
- Brush with ½ the barbecue sauce. Close the lid and grill for 5 to 10 minutes, monitoring closely for flare-ups.
- Turn and baste the other side with more BBQ sauce.
- Close the lid and grill, (again, watching for flare-ups). Cook for an additional 5 to 10 minutes.
- Keep turning and basting until the ribs reach your desired color.
- Slice rib racks into portions and add additional barbecue sauce when serving, if desired.

INGREDIENTS

prep time: 10 mins | total time: 1.5 hrs | servings: ten

- **5 lbs** boneless Boston Butt
- **2 cups** broth of choice
- **1 (1 oz) packet** ranch seasoning
- **2 tsp** salt
- **4 whole** garlic cloves
- **2 tsp** cumin
- **4** sliced fresh jalapeños, seeded
- **¼ cup** golden monk fruit
- **2 tsp** paprika
- **1** white onion, peeled & quartered
- **1 tbsp** Worcestershire sauce
- Optional: **1** lime, juiced

Carnitas

DIRECTIONS

- Place pork, all seasonings, onion, garlic, and jalapeno to a pressure cooker.
- Stir together broth, sauce, monk fruit, and lime juice in a small bowl until mixed well. Pour into pressure cooker over the pork.
- Cook for 1 hour and 15 minutes. When done, allow the pressure to release naturally for about 10 minutes.
- Remove the vegetables, shred the meat, and reserve 1 cup of the juice (minimum).

Continued on next page.

DIRECTIONS

- Place shredded meat in a single layer on baking sheet or in a casserole dish.
- Broil meat on high 2-3 minutes or until crisp.
- Keep a close eye on the tray as it broils, all ovens vary in power/temperature. Try to take the tray out as soon as the mean looks lightly browned and crispy!
- Take meat out of oven and spoon some of the juice over the top of the meat. This helps make the meat super flavorful and moist, so don't skip!
- Serve carnitas with warm low-carb tortillas, lime wedges, and keto slaw.
- Alternatively, you can serve with your salad of choice.

INGREDIENTS

 prep time: 20 mins    total time: 1 hr - 1 day    servings: four

- **14 oz** gluten-free pork sausage meat
- **6 oz** chicken liver, finely chopped
- **1 cup** grated Parmesan cheese
- **1** large egg
- **2 tbsp** ghee (can sub virgin olive or avocado oil)
- **¼ cup** fresh parsley
- Salt and pepper, **to taste**

Cheesy Sausage Liver Meatballs

DIRECTIONS

- For a milder tasting liver, place in a bowl filled with 2 cups of cold water and 1-2 tbsp of lemon juice and refrigerate for at least 30 minutes or overnight.
- Preheat oven to 465 °F and dice the chicken liver into small pieces.
- Place the sausage meat, liver, egg, cheese, fresh parsley, salt and pepper in a bowl. Mix until combined.
- Form 18-22 medium sized meatballs and spread evenly on a greased or lined baking tray. Do not overcrowd.
- Drizzle with melted ghee (or oil). Bake for 10 to 15 minutes, turn the meatballs, and bake for an additional 10-15 minutes, until golden brown and cooked through.
- Serve with low-carb sides or salad of choice. It's also great for lunch-on-the-go with fresh veggies and some oil of choice.
- Serve warm or let them cool down and refrigerate for up to 4 days.
- You can also freeze these meatballs for up to 3 months!

INGREDIENTS

prep time: 10 mins
total time: 25 mins
servings: six (6)

- **6** small hot dogs/sausages, cut in half (or 12 cocktail wieners)
- **1 ½ cups** grated cheese
- **⅔ cup** almond flour
- **2 tbsp** melted butter
- **½ tsp** Italian seasoning
- **¼ tsp** garlic powder
- **¼ tsp** onion powder

Pigs in a Blanket

DIRECTIONS

- Preheat oven to 400 °F.
- For the **dough**: melt the cheese in a microwave in 30 second increments until just melted, but not brown or crispy.
- Slowly stir in the almond flour and mix well. As it thickens, don't be afraid to get your hands involved - get a little messy!
- Once formed, roll it out between 2 sheets of wax paper and fold in half to create a long strip of dough. Cut down the middle, then repeat until you have similar sized portioned strips.
- In a small bowl, combine melted butter with herbs, garlic and onion powder. Brush each slice with the butter, place a sausage on each one and wrap the dough around tightly. Pinch to close and brush any leftover butter on top.
- Place (pinched side down) on a tray and bake for 15 to 20 minutes.
- Remove from the oven and set aside to cool down slightly.
- Enjoy warm or store in the fridge, once fully cooled, for up to 3 days.
- Serve with desired K2 friendly toppings.

INGREDIENTS

 prep time: 2-24 hrs
 total time: 5 hrs - 1 day +
 servings: four

- **1 lb** pork tenderloin
- **¼ cup** yellow mustard
- **1 tbsp** salt
- **1 tbsp** pepper
- **1 tbsp** garlic powder
- **1 tbsp** chili powder
- **1 tsp** oregano dried
- **1 tsp** parsley dried
- Hickory wood chips/pellets (or alternative)

Pork Tenderloin

DIRECTIONS

- Remove fat and tough 'silver skin' from the tenderloin. Coat in mustard.
- Combine spices in a bowl and massage evenly over the tenderloin.
- Wrap the tenderloin in plastic wrap and place in refrigerator for 2-24 hours (the longer it sits, the more flavor!)
- Remove and allow to reach room temperature before cooking.
- Start smoker with wood of your choice and set to 200°F.
- Heat a large pan or skillet and sear pork tenderloin on all sides, on high heat.
- Place pork tenderloin on smoker. Smoke until internal temperature reaches 145°F for medium rare and 160°F for medium (about 2-3 hours, time will vary depending on your equipment. Always best to use a thermometer to read the internal temperature!)
- Remove pork tenderloin from heat and let rest 10-15 minutes.
- Slice and serve as desired.

INGREDIENTS

prep time: 20 mins | total time: 20 mins | servings: six

- **4 lbs** boneless pork shoulder
- **1 cup** beef bone broth
- **¼ cup** apple cider vinegar
- **¼ cup** coconut aminos
- **1** medium onion, diced
- **1 tbsp** olive oil
- **1 tbsp** salt
- **1 tbsp** smoked paprika
- **2 tsp** garlic powder
- **1 tsp** cumin
- **1 tsp** cayenne pepper
- **½ tsp** blackstrap molasses

Pulled Pork

DIRECTIONS

- Trim the fat off of the pork and pat dry with paper towel. Season all sides with smoked paprika, salt, garlic powder, cumin, and cayenne.
- Massage with your hands and let sit for 20 minutes.
- Heat the oil in a large Dutch oven over medium-high heat. Add the pork and sear for 1-2 minutes per side, until browned.
- While the pork is browning, place the onion into the slow cooker.
- Combine broth, coconut aminos, vinegar, and molasses in a bowl.
- Place the pork roast into the slow cooker. Pour the broth mixture **around** the pork (not directly on top).
- Cook for 10-12 hours on low, until pork pulls apart easily.
- Gently shred the pork with two forks and strain excess liquid before serving.

KETO 2.0

APPROVED

Fish & Seafood Recipes

INGREDIENTS

prep time: 2 mins
total time: 5 mins
servings: twelve (12)

- **1 lb** fresh tuna, sushi grade
- **1** avocado chopped
- **1 tsp** ginger
- **1 ½ tbsp** soy sauce
- **1 tsp** lime juice
- **2 tbsp** lime juice
- **1 ½ tbsp** sesame oil
- **⅛ tsp** salt & pepper

Tuna Tartare

DIRECTIONS

- Slice the tuna into ¼-inch cubes (or desired shape and size) and place them in a mixing bowl.
- In a separate bowl, whisk together the ginger, soy sauce, lime juice and sesame oil until combined.
- Pour the sauce over the tuna and gently mix until incorporated.
- Place the chopped avocado in the bottom of a small glass bowl.
- Squeeze some lime juice on top. Add salt and pepper to taste.
- Place tuna on top of avocado.
- Alternatively, you can place it on cucumber slices or lettuce boats for appetizers.

Optional garnish:
- Finely sliced green onion (or chives) and/or 1 tbsp sesame seeds.

INGREDIENTS

 prep time: 15 mins   total time: 5 mins  servings: six

- **3.5 oz** oysters, shucked (approximately 12 oysters)
- **1 large** egg
- **¼ cup** almond flour super-fine
- **¼ cup** Parmesan cheese, grated
- Salt and pepper, to taste
- **Cooking oil** of your choice, for frying

Fried Oysters

DIRECTIONS

- Shuck oysters. and place them on a paper towel. Pat dry.
- Mix almond flour and Parmesan cheese together in a bowl.
- In a separate, smaller bowl, beat the egg.
- One at a time, lightly coat an oyster in the flour and Parmesan mixture. Transfer the oyster into the eggs, then back to the flour.
- Set aside until the remaining oysters have been coated.
- Heat your cooking oil in a large pot (for frying) over medium-high heat.
- Once bubbling, gently place the oysters into the oil.
- Fry each side of the oyster until slightly golden.
- If the oil is not deep enough for the oysters to float, be extra careful when turning the oysters to prevent the cheese in the breading from sticking to the pan.
- Transfer the oysters to a plate with some paper towels to absorb excess oil before serving.

INGREDIENTS

prep time: 5 mins

total time: 30 mins

servings: two

- **2 eggs**, lightly beaten
- **1** package Shirataki/Konjac Pasta
- **1 ½ tbsp** fish sauce
- **1 ½ tbsp** coconut aminos
- **2 tbsp** xylitol or erythritol
- **⅛-¼ tsp** pepper flakes, to taste
- **2-3** tbsp lime juice, to taste
- **1-2 tbsp** coconut oil, for cooking
- **2 cloves** garlic, minced
- **200 g** fresh shrimp or chicken
- **30 g** bean sprouts
- **¼ tsp** blackstrap molasses (can sub **1 tsp** brown sugar)

Shrimp Pad Thai

DIRECTIONS

- Follow your brand's cooking instructions for the shirataki noodles instructions. Set aside. (Can sub your favorite K2 friendly noodles.)
- In a small bowl whisk fish sauce, coconut aminos, sweetener and red pepper flakes or cayenne.
- Slowly add the lime juice, starting with 2 tbsp, adjusting to taste.
- Heat oil in a skillet or pan on medium heat. Add in garlic and sauté until it just begins to brown.

Continued on next page.

SHRIMP PAD THAI, CONTINUED

- Add the shrimp and cook for 2-5 minutes on each side, until just cooked through. Move the shrimp to the edges of the pan.
- Gently beat the eggs and add to the pan, stirring them to scramble.
- Pour in the sauce and mix just long enough for the shrimp and eggs to be evenly coated.
- Add in noodles, bean sprouts and continue to cook for an additional 2-3 minutes.
- If desired, garnish with green onions, cilantro and peanuts.
- Serve immediately with fresh lime.

Optional Garnish:
- Sliced green onions and/or fresh cilantro
- 35 g toasted and unsalted chopped peanuts
- Lime wedges

INGREDIENTS

 prep time: 10 mins   total time: 25 mins  servings: four

- **1 bag** Cauliflower Rice
- **1 lb** raw shrimp; peeled, deveined
- **1 ½ cups** cashews soaked overnight
- **1 bag** Mann's Kohlrabi Linguine
- **2 tbsp** olive oil
- **4 cloves** garlic minced
- **1 ½ cups** plain unsweetened almond milk
- **3 tbsp** nutritional yeast
- **1 tbsp** lemon juice
- **Garlic pepper** to taste
- **Salt** and **pepper** to taste
- **2** green onion stems
- **2 tbsp** butter

Alfredo Shrimp Pasta

DIRECTIONS

- Prepare cauliflower rice according to the bag's directions. Set aside.
- In a medium pan, heat the olive oil over medium heat and add the garlic. Sauté, stirring occasionally until golden.
- Transfer to a blender with the cauliflower rice, almond milk, cashews, nutritional yeast, and lemon juice. Purée until very smooth and season with salt and pepper.

Continued on next page.

ALFREDO SHRIMP PASTA, CONTINUED

- Add 2 tbsp of butter to a heavy skillet over medium heat.
- Add the shrimp to the skillet and sprinkle with salt, pepper, and garlic pepper.
- Cook, stirring occasionally, for 4-5 minutes or until shrimp is cooked through. Remove shrimp and set aside.
- Return the medium pan to the heat and add the bag of Mann's Kohlrabi Linguine.
- Sauté until softened, approximately 5-7 minutes. Pour in the sauce and stir to combine.
- Add shrimp and toss all ingredients until fully coated.
- Divide between plates and sprinkle with chopped green onions or desired garnish.

INGREDIENTS

prep time: 10 mins | total time: 20 mins | servings: four

- **1 lb** shrimp deveined
- **1 tbsp** garlic infused olive oil (**1 tbsp** olive oil & ¼ tsp garlic powder)
- **1 tsp** Old Bay seasoning
- **¼ cup** butter
- **1 clove** garlic minced
- **1 tbsp** fresh parsley minced
- Salt, **to taste**
- Ground pepper, **to taste**
- 1 lemon, squeezed for garnish

Shrimp Skewers

DIRECTIONS

- Preheat grill or barbeque on low heat.
- Toss shrimp with olive oil, salt, pepper, and Old Bay. Put on skewers.
- Lay shrimp on smoker rack in a single layer and close the lid.
- Check shrimp after 10 minutes and keep a close eye on them.
- Smoke shrimp until just cooked through, about 15-20 minutes total.
- While shrimp are smoking, stir together butter, garlic, herbs and salt to taste in a small bowl.
- Drizzle over cooked shrimp and toss to coat.
- Serve the remaining garlic herb butter mixture as a dipping sauce.
- Drizzle with lemon juice and enjoy!

INGREDIENTS

prep time: 10 mins | total time: 20 mins | servings: four

Batter
- **1 cup** almond flour
- **2** eggs
- **½ cup** unsweetened full-fat **coconut milk**

Breading
- **½ cup** almond flour
- **1 ½ cup** unsweetened shredded coconut
- **1 tsp** salt
- **1 tsp** cayenne pepper
- **1 tsp** garlic powder
- **1 lb** shrimp
- **1-2 cups** refined coconut oil for frying

Dipping Sauce
- **¼ cup** mayo
- **¼ cup** sour cream or plain yogurt or
- **1 tbsp** Thai chili garlic sauce
- **1 tsp** white wine vinegar or rice wine vinegar
- **2 tbsp** lime juice
- **1 tsp** granular erythritol

Coconut Shrimp

DIRECTIONS

- Combine all batter ingredients in a bowl.
- In a separate bowl, mix all the breading ingredients together.
- Peel, devein, and leave the tails on the shrimp.
- Coat the shrimp in the batter, shake off any excess, and then coat the shrimp in the dry mixture. Shake off the excess again.
- Place the coated shrimp on a plate and repeat the same process for all of the remaining shrimp.
- Heat the coconut oil in a cast-iron skillet to 360°F.
- Carefully place the shrimp in the hot oil in small batches (do not overcrowd) and cook for 2-3 minutes.
- Transfer the shrimp to a plate and pat with paper towel to soak up any extra oil before serving.

INGREDIENTS

prep time: 5 mins
total time: 25 mins
servings: two

- **1 lb** salmon, boneless fillets, cut into desired sizes
- **1 tbsp** butter, or oil of choice
- **1 tbsp** lemon juice
- Salt and ground black pepper **to taste**
- **2 tsp** finely chopped fresh chives or fresh dill

Lemon Salmon

DIRECTIONS

- Combine all batter ingredients in a bowl.
- In a separate bowl, mix all the breading ingredients together.
- Peel, devein, and leave the tails on the shrimp.
- Coat the shrimp in the batter, shake off any excess, and then coat the shrimp in the dry mixture. Shake off the excess again.
- Place the coated shrimp on a plate and repeat the same process for all of the remaining shrimp.
- Heat the refined coconut oil in a cast-iron skillet to 360°F.
- Carefully place the shrimp in the hot oil in small batches (do not overcrowd) and cook for 2-3 minutes.
- Transfer the shrimp to a plate and pat with paper towel to soak up any extra oil before serving.

INGREDIENTS

 prep time: 15 mins   total time: 20 mins  servings: four

- **25 grams (4 slices)** Salmon
- **2 cups** of cauliflower rice
- **2** pieces of nori sheets
- **1 medium** zucchini (can sub cucumber)
- **1 tbsp** of Vinegar
- **1** Stevia tablet (or sweetener of choice)
- **½** medium avocado

Avocado Salmon Sushi

DIRECTIONS

- Get all of your ingredients ready, slicing as desired. Make sure to sure fresh salmon if possible; it makes for a much tastier sushi!
- Prepare cauliflower rice according to instructions (or use my recipe here)
- Place the cauliflower onto a bowl and prepare your Nori sheets.
- Once your Nori sheet is prepared, add the cauli rice as you would in traditional sushi making.
- Add your desired veggies with the salmon at the very end of the sheets. Lightly wet the edges of the nori with water so it will hold once rolled.
- Tightly roll the sushi and place it aside. Follow the same instructions for the second roll.
- Once rolled, use a sharp knife to portion the sushi and plate for serving.

INGREDIENTS

 prep time: 5 mins  total time: 15 mins  servings: six

- **1 (6 oz)** can lump crab meat
- **¼ cup** mayonnaise
- **1** egg
- **2 tbsp** chopped green onions
- **1 tsp** lime juice
- **½ tsp** lime zest
- **½ tsp** Old Bay seasoning
- **1 ¼** cup pork rind panko crumbs (see notes below)

Crab Cakes

DIRECTIONS

- In a mixing bowl combine all of the ingredients and chill for 10 minutes to allow the mixture to thicken slightly and the flavors time to meld.
- Heat a large heavy bottom skillet to medium heat. Add 2-3 tbsp oil.
- Scoop out about ¼ cup of the mixture at a time and form into a patty.
- Place in the skillet. Cook 3-4 minutes on each side until crispy.
- Remove from the skillet and dab off grease with paper towel.

NOTES

So, what's "pork rind panko" and how do I use it? You may be familiar with panko style breadcrumbs, made from crustless-bread and have signature large, airy flakes. These breadcrumbs are difficult to incorporate on a keto diet, so pork rind panko is an excellent substitute!

INGREDIENTS

 prep time: 5 mins total time: 25 mins  servings: eight

- **1 lb.** crab meat
- **8 oz.** softened cream cheese
- **¼ cup** mayo
- **¼ cup** sour cream
- **⅛ cup** feta cheese
- **1 tsp** Worcestershire sauce
- **1 tsp** Old Bay Seasoning (plus more to garnish)
- **¼ tsp** garlic powder
- **¼ tsp** onion powder
- **½ cup** shredded cheddar cheese (plus **¼ cup** for topping)
- Parsley, chives, or scallions, chopped, for garnish
- Salt and pepper, **to taste**

Crab Dip

DIRECTIONS

- Preheat oven to 350°F.
- Let the sour cream and cream cheese soften at room temperature before using.
- Mix all ingredients (except crab) in a bowl.
- Once thoroughly combined, gently fold in the crab meat.
- Pour the mixture into a lightly greased or line casserole dish and evenly sprinkle some extra cheese on top.
- Serve with K2 friendly pretzels or low carb crackers/chips.

INGREDIENTS

prep time: 10 mins
total time: 15 mins
servings: four

- **16 ounces** sea scallops
- **8 slices** bacon
- **1 tbsp** butter
- **1 tsp** minced garlic
- **½ tsp** Old Bay seasoning (to taste)
- Salt and pepper **to taste**
- **Lemon** slices/juice optional

Bacon Wrapped Scallops

DIRECTIONS

- Preheat the oven to 400°F.
- Rinse the scallops thoroughly and pat dry with a paper towel.
- Cut bacon slices in half and gently stretch them out - this will help the bacon keep its shape, and not shrink as much as it cooks.
- If you prefer crispy bacon, pre-cook the bacon in the preheated oven on a baking sheet for 6-10 minutes. Pat dry.
- Wrap bacon slice around the scallop, secure with a toothpick or skewer and place on a greased baking sheet.
- In a small bowl combine the melted butter, minced garlic and Old Bay seasoning.
- Brush the mixture on each scallop, coating evenly.
- Bake for 10-12 minutes until the bacon is crisp and the scallop tender, flipping halfway for a more even cook.
- **Optional**: garnish with lemon slices and/or a few squirts of lemon juice when serving.

INGREDIENTS

prep time: 5 mins
total time: 25 mins
servings: four

- **2 (8 oz)** packages Baby Bella Mushrooms
- **4 oz** cream cheese (room temperature)
- **1 (6 ounce)** can lump crab meat, drained
- **1 cup** shredded cheese. (Havarti, mozzarella, gruyere or Parmesan for a stronger taste)
- **4 slices** thick bacon, cooked and chopped
- **Optional garnish**: cilantro, parsley or any desired herbs/spices

Crab & Bacon Stuffed Mushrooms

DIRECTIONS

- Preheat the oven to 350 °F.
- Spray a medium size baking sheet with cooking oil and set aside.
- Wash mushroom caps thoroughly, remove and discard the stems, and place mushrooms on the baking sheet mushroom cap down.
- In a small bowl, combine the cream cheese, crab, shredded cheese, and chopped bacon.
- Spoonful enough of the mixture to fill each mushroom your desired amount.
- Bake for 18-20 minutes. Let cool before serving.

INGREDIENTS

 prep time: 2 mins  total time: 10 mins   yield: four cups

- **1 ¼ cup** half & half cream
- **2 cups** sharp cheddar cheese
- **1 (10-oz)** can diced tomatoes
- Green chilies, **to taste**
- **½ tsp** cayenne pepper
- **¼ tsp** onion powder
- **¼ tsp** garlic powder
- **½ tsp** turmeric
- **½ tsp** salt
- **Optional Garnish**:
- **¼ tsp** paprika
- **1 tbsp** of parmesan cheese

Queso 2.0

What's better than queso? **Homemade** queso with some **extra flavor**!

DIRECTIONS

- Add the half & half to a small pot and gradually heat, just until it starts to simmer; stir occasionally.
- Remove the pan from the heat and add in the cayenne, onion powder, garlic powder, salt and turmeric and stir until combined.
- Add in the sharp cheddar cheese and stir until combined and the cheese is melted. Stir in the can of diced tomatoes and chopped green chilies to taste.
- Serve warm with your favorite keto-friendly dippers!
- **Optional**: Sprinkle paprika and parmesan cheese over the top.

INGREDIENTS

prep time: 5 mins | total time: 10 mins | servings: 10 ten

- 4 large, ripe avocados
- 2 **tbsp** sour cream
- 1 roma tomato
- ½ red onion
- 1 **clove** garlic
- ½ jalapeno pepper
- ¼ **cup** cilantro
- 1 lime
- 1 **tsp** cumin
- Salt and pepper **to taste**

Guacamole

Have some fun with this super simple and nutrition packed recipe! Feel free to get creative in switching up the veggies - there are no steadfast rules here!

DIRECTIONS

- Wash and prepare all ingredients, finely slicing the vegetables in any desired shape and size.
- Cut the avocados length wise and scoop the flesh into a bowl. Mash avocados with a fork (or mortar and pestle).
- Mix in remainder of ingredients.
- You can substitute lemon instead of lime if desired, and either citrus fruit helps to keep your guacamole fresh and green!

INGREDIENTS

prep time: 15 mins | total time: 1 hr 15 mins | yield: 4 cups

- **10 oz** frozen spinach
- **1 ¼ cups** sour cream
- **¾ cup** mayonnaise
- **½ tsp** gluten-free Worcestershire sauce
- **2 tsp** onion powder
- **1 tsp** minced garlic (can sub dried/powdered garlic)
- **1 tsp** salt
- Pepper, to taste

Spinach Dip

DIRECTIONS

- Thaw the frozen spinach and squeeze as much water out as you can. You can use paper towel or cheesecloth if needed.
- Finely chop up the spinach - even if your frozen spinach is pre-chopped you can do some additional chopping; the spinach stems can become stringy if left whole.
- In a small mixing bowl, combine mayonnaise and sour cream.
- Add in the Worcestershire sauce, onion powder, minced garlic, salt, and pepper.
- Stir in the spinach and mix until everything is combined.
- Chill for at least an hour before serving with your favorite K2 friendly dippers.

INGREDIENTS

 prep time: 20 mins   total time: 25 mins   yield: 8 cups

- 1 ½ **lbs** roma tomatoes (or similar)
- ⅓ **cup** chopped red onion
- 1 jalapeno pepper, seeded and roughly chopped
- ⅓ **cup** fresh chopped cilantro
- 1 **clove** garlic, roughly chopped
- 3 **tbsp** fresh squeezed lime juice
- 1 **tsp** salt and pepper to taste
- ½ **tsp** chili powder
- ¼ **tsp** ground cumin

Salsa

Here is another super simple but delicious recipe. Feel free to switch up the ingredients as desired, just keep it K2 friendly!

DIRECTIONS

- Slice and prepare all ingredients as desired.
- Combine all ingredients into a food processor.
- Pulse for 10-30 seconds until desired consistency is reached.
- Serve right away or store in the refrigerator for up to four days.

INGREDIENTS

 prep time: 5 mins   total time: 20 mins   servings: sixteen

- **1 cup** beef bone broth
- **6 oz** tomato paste
- **3 tbsp** apple cider vinegar
- **1 tbsp** Swerve sweetener
- **1 tsp** garlic powder
- **1 tsp** onion powder
- **1 tsp** dry mustard
- **1 tsp** sea salt
- **⅛ tsp** ground cinnamon
- **⅛ tsp** cayenne pepper

Ketchup

DIRECTIONS

- Combine all ingredients in a small saucepan on medium heat.
- Bring to a simmer, and reduce heat to medium low.
- Cook for 15 minutes, then allow to cool completely. Store sealed in the refrigerator for up to one week.

Tomatoes are more than acceptable on a K2 diet, so ketchup should be too, right? Unfortunately, most big brands add a TON of sugar to their products (which increases the number of carbs). One tbsp of typical store-brand ketchup contains 4g of carbs... and most people eat more than that a time. Pay attention to the labels; there are several low sugar, keto-friendly brands out there. Alternatively, you can use the recipe above to make your own! Homemade is always the best option if it works for you because you know exactly what you'll be putting in your body.

INGREDIENTS

 prep time: 5 mins   total time: 10 mins   16 servings: sixteen

- **1 cup** oil (ideally extra virgin olive oil, coconut or avocado oil)
- **1 tbsp** apple cider vinegar
- **1** egg

Mayonnaise

DIRECTIONS

- Combine the egg and vinegar in a blender or food processor
- While still blending, slowly pour in the oil. You should hear a change in the blender sound when you've added enough oil - then it will thicken quite quickly
- Can be stored in the fridge for up to one week
- Optional: lemon juice or your favorite spices (try chipotle or hot sauce for an extra kick!

While mayonnaise won't knock your body out of ketosis, many store brands contain potentially harmful ingredients that can trigger inflammation (among other things). Ingredients to look out for are: **artificial** preservatives, **MSG** and **vegetable** oils.

There are some keto-friendly brands out there so pay attention to the nutrition label before buying - or use the recipe above to make your own!

INGREDIENTS

 prep time: 10 mins   total time: 10 mins    servings: twenty

- **1 cup** water
- **6 oz** tomato paste
- **¼ cup** apple cider vinegar
- **¼ cup** brown sugar (or substitute)
- **½ tsp** garlic powder
- **1 tsp** liquid smoke
- **1 tsp** smoked paprika
- **½ tsp** onion powder
- **½ tsp** cumin
- **1 tsp** salt
- **1 tsp** pepper
- **½ tsp** minced garlic

Barbeque Sauce

DIRECTIONS

- In a small saucepan, add all your ingredients and mix well.
- On medium heat, heat up the saucepan until it begins to simmer.
- Once it begins to simmer, reduce to very low and stir for 4-5 minutes.
- Remove from the heat and let cool completely.
- Sauce will thicken as it cools.
- Store sealed in the fridge for one week.

INGREDIENTS

prep time: 2 mins
total time: 12 mins
servings: sixteen — 16

- **2 cups** raw hazelnuts
- **3 tbsp** allulose
- **2 tbsp** cocoa powder
- Nutmilk bag or cheesecloth

Nutella

DIRECTIONS

- Preheat the oven to 350°F.
- Line a pan with the hazelnuts in a single layer, and toast for 12-15 minutes.
- Allow hazelnuts to cool completely and transfer to a nutmilk bag (can use a large cheesecloth, holding all corners together to form a bag).
- Using one hand, press and shake the hazelnuts together roughly, to remove the skins.
- After a couple of minutes, the skins should easily fall off to discard.
- Place the skinned hazelnuts into a high-speed blender or food processor and blend for 4-5 minutes
- Once it is a flour-like consistency, stir through using a rubber spatula and blend until smooth and creamy.
- Add your cocoa powder and granulated sweetener and continue to blend until fully combined and silky smooth.
- Transfer your chocolate hazelnut spread into a jar or container.
- Store in the fridge for up to one week.

INGREDIENTS

 prep time: 2 mins  total time: 10 mins  servings: six

- **1 cup** heavy whipping cream
- **¼ cup** butter or ghee
- **2 tbsp mascarpone**
- **1 clove** garlic minced
- **½ tsp** basil, dried
- **½ tsp** oregano, dried
- **½ tsp** parsley, dried
- **½ cup** parmesan cheese, grated
- Salt and pepper, **to taste**
- Warm water (optional)

Alfredo Sauce

DIRECTIONS

- Combine butter, heavy whipping cream, and mascarpone in a saucepan over low medium heat.
- Reduce to low heat and simmer for 2 to 3 minutes.
- Add garlic, basil, oregano, and parsley. Stir just to combine and then take off heat.
- Whisk sauce well. Slowly incorporate the Parmesan cheese and whisk until thoroughly melted and combined.
- Season with salt and pepper, to taste.
- If sauce becomes thicker than preferred, slowly whisk in a small amount of warm water to reach desired consistency.
- Best used immediately but can be stored tightly sealed in the fridge for 2-3 days.

INGREDIENTS

 prep time: 10 mins  total time: 10 mins   **8**  servings: eight

- **1 large** cucumber
- **1.65 lbs** Greek yogurt
- **Zest** and **juice** from 1 lemon
- **3 cloves** garlic, crushed
- **4 tbsp** finely chopped dill
- **4 tbsp** finely chopped mint
- **⅓ cup** extra virgin olive oil
- **¾ tsp** sea salt
- **½ tsp** black pepper

Greek Tzatziki

DIRECTIONS

- Start by grating the cucumber.
- Transfer just the grated cucumber to a bowl with yogurt; do not pour in the cucumber juices or it will be too runny.
- For a thicker Tzatziki, squeeze out some of the cucumber juice with paper towel before adding to the bowl with yogurt.
- Add the lemon juice and zest, crushed garlic, chopped dill and mint.
- Add the olive oil and season with salt and pepper to taste. Stir well to combine.
- Drizzle the remaining olive oil on top and optionally garnish with more herbs and black pepper.
- Serve immediately as a dip or side dish.
- To store, place in a sealable container, cover with a lid and store in the fridge for up to 4 days.

INGREDIENTS

 prep time: 5 mins  total time: 15 mins  servings: twelve

- ½ **cup** mayonnaise
- ½ **cup** sour cream
- ¼ **cup** heavy cream (+ ¼ **cup** extra for thinning, if needed)
- 1 **tsp** apple cider vinegar
- 1 **tsp** dried oregano
- 1 **tsp** garlic powder
- 1 **tsp** onion powder
- 1 **tsp** sea salt
- ½ **tsp** dried dill
- ½ **tsp** ground black pepper
- Broth optional - **for thinning**

Ranch

DIRECTIONS

- Combine ¼ cup cream and apple cider vinegar in a medium bowl and whisk until combined.
- Allow it to rest on your counter for at least 10 minutes.
- Add all remaining ingredients to the bowl, whisking until thoroughly combined.
- Thin to desired consistency using more heavy cream or bone broth. For a ranch dip, keep the consistency thicker. For a ranch dressing or sauce, thin it out slightly.
- Transfer to an airtight container and store in the fridge for up to one week.

INGREDIENTS

 prep time: 5 mins
 total time: 2 hrs 5 mins
 servings: sixteen

- **1 cup** sour cream
- **¾ cup** mayonnaise
- **2 oz** softened cream cheese
- **1 ½ tbsp** fresh dill
- **1 tbsp** dried chives
- **½ tsp** salt
- **½ tsp** pepper
- **½ tsp** onion powder
- **½ tsp** ground celery seed
- **2** cloves minced garlic
- **½** lemon squeezed

Dill Veggie Dip

DIRECTIONS

- Combine all of the ingredients into a serving bowl.
- Cover and refrigerate for at least 2 hours.
- Serve with any preferred vegetables.

It doesn't get much simpler than that!

KETO 2.0

APPROVED

Sweets & Deserts Recipes

INGREDIENTS

 prep time: 5 mins　 total time: 55 mins　 servings: eight

- **6** large eggs
- **1 ½ cups** coconut flour sifted
- **1 ½ cups** arrowroot flour
- **1 tbsp** baking soda
- **1 tbsp** baking powder
- **½ tsp** salt
- **⅔ cup** coconut oil melted
- **1 ½ cups** maple syrup can sub honey
- **1 ½ cups** cocoa powder
- **1 ½ cups** milk of choice
- **1 tbsp** vanilla extract
- **1-2 cups** K2 friendly chocolate frosting

Chocolate Cake

DIRECTIONS

- Preheat the oven to 350°F. Grease 3 separate 8-inch cake pans and set aside.
- In a mixing bowl, combine all dry ingredients, except cocoa powder.
- In a separate bowl, combine your coconut oil, maple syrup, and cocoa powder.
- Whisk eggs in separate small bowl and slowly pour in, until combined.
- Add the milk and vanilla extract and whisk together, until combined.
- Gently fold in the dry ingredients and mix until thick.

CHOCOLATE CAKE, CONTINUED

- Pour the batter evenly into the three cake pans. Bake for 25-30 minutes, or until a fork comes out mostly clean.
- Remove from the oven and let them cool completely in their pans.
- Once cool, cut the tops off of two cakes so they are completely flat.
- Spread frosting on both of those cakes, and then stack one on the other.
- Spread with more frosting, before adding the final rounded-top layer.
- Spread the top with the remaining frosting, along with the entire exterior.
- Let the cake sit for 20 minutes, before serving.
- Get creative with how you decorate it!

INGREDIENTS

 prep time: 5 mins
 total time: 40 mins
 servings: twelve

- **3** large eggs
- **1 ½ cups** almond flour
- **1 tsp** baking powder
- **½ tsp** salt
- **6 tbsp** butter softened
- **1 ¾ cups** granulated sweetener of your choosing (white, brown, coconut, sugar free, etc.)
- **¾ cup** cocoa powder
- **1 tsp** vanilla extract
- **½ cup** chocolate chips (optional)

Brownies

DIRECTIONS

- Preheat the oven to 350°F. Lightly grease or line an 8-inch pan with parchment paper. Set aside.
- In a small bowl, stir together all dry ingredients.
- In a separate (larger) bowl, whisk the eggs, softened butter, sweetener, cocoa powder, and vanilla extract, until combined.
- Slowly add in your dry ingredients and mix until fully combined.
- If using chocolate chips, gently fold them through last.
- Transfer your brownie batter into the pan and bake for about 35 minutes, or until a toothpick or fork comes out clean.
- Remove from the oven and allow to cool completely, before slicing.
- Store in the fridge for 4-5 days (if you have leftovers).

INGREDIENTS

 prep time: 5 mins   total time: 6+ hrs    servings: four

- **1 cup** almond milk (or similar)
- **¼ cup** chia seeds
- **1 tsp** cinnamon
- **1 ripe** banana
- **1 tbsp** chopped walnuts for garnish

Banana Chai Pudding

This dish makes an excellent healthy desert, but it can also be enjoyed as breakfast or a snack on the go! If you aren't a fan of bananas, or would prefer a lower carb fruit, get creative! Chia pudding is extremely versatile, so you can switch up the ingredients you use quite easily.

DIRECTIONS

- Combine 1 cup almond milk, ¼ cup chia seeds, and 1 tsp cinnamon into a medium bowl. Stir and refrigerate overnight or at least 6 hours
- Note: for better consistency you can stir chia seeds once after 30 minutes and again after another 30 minutes before letting them rest for the full 6 hours.
- Divide into 4 servings after refrigeration (mason jars work great!)
- Top each serving with ¼ banana, sliced and 1 tbsp of chopped walnuts if desired (or other preferred topping).

INGREDIENTS

prep time: 15 mins | total time: 8 hrs | servings: four (4)

- **2 tbsp** water
- **¾ cup** heavy whipping cream or full fat coconut milk
- **2** large eggs
- **½ cup** unsweetened almond or cashew milk
- **¼ cup + 3 tbsp** Allulose, divided
- **1 tbsp** additional sweetener of choice
- **1 tsp** sugar-free vanilla extract
- **Optional garnish**: vanilla beans

Crème Caramel

DIRECTIONS

- **Caramel sauce**: pour ¼ cup of Allulose in a pot filled with water. Bring to a light boil and cover with a lid for 10 to 15 minutes, until it starts to thicken and brown slightly. Add additional allulose if required to reach desired consistency. Remove from heat.
- Preheat the oven to 350°F.
- Divide the mixture between 4 ramekins and place on a baking tray.
- Add hot water to the tray (enough to be ¼ inch full)

Continued on next page.

CRÈME CARAMEL, CONTINUED

- Pour the eggs, whipping cream (or coconut milk), almond milk, sweetener, and vanilla extract into a blender.
- Process until smooth but not frothy (avoid having too many bubbles) and pour into ramekins, on top of the caramel.
- Place the tray in the oven and bake for 20 to 25 minutes. Rotate the tray and bake for an additional 20 minutes.
- Remove from the oven and set aside to fully cool down at room temperature.
- Cover and refrigerate overnight.
- When ready to serve, use a sharp knife around the edges to release the crème caramel and transfer to a plate.
- Can be stored covered tightly in the fridge for up to 4 days.

INGREDIENTS

prep time: 10 mins
total time: 30 mins
servings: six

- **2 ¼ cups** almond flour
- **2** large eggs
- **½ tsp** baking soda
- **½ tsp** salt
- **3 tbsp** avocado oil (or oil of choice)
- **1 tbsp** K2 friendly maple syrup (or similar)
- **1 tsp** vanilla extract
- **Whipping cream** or alternative
- **Strawberries**, of course!

Strawberry Shortcake

DIRECTIONS

- Preheat the oven to 350°F.
- Line a baking sheet with parchment paper; set aside.
- In a medium mixing bowl, combine all dry ingredients.
- Add eggs, oil, syrup, and vanilla and stir until combined.
- Scoop ¼ cup of dough and use your hands to form a round shortcake - about 2 inches thick.
- Place each one onto the prepared baking sheet and press down slightly. Repeat until all dough is used, and do not overcrowd.
- Bake for 15 -17 minutes or until the centers are cooked and the tops start to crack. Remove from the oven and let cool completely.
- When serving, top each shortcake with a pile of strawberries and a spoonful of K2 friendly whipped cream, or similar.
- Best served right away but can be stored in the refrigerator for 2-3 days.

INGREDIENTS

prep time: 10 mins total time: 40 mins servings: ten

- ½ **cup** vanilla or plain K2 friendly protein powder
- ¾ **cup** creamy almond butter (all natural)
- ¼ **cup** honey
- 1 **tbsp** melted coconut oil
- ⅓ **cup** ground flaxseed meal
- 2.5 **oz** K2 friendly dark chocolate bar
- 1 **tsp** vanilla

Chocolate Almond Protein Bars

DIRECTIONS

- Combine almond butter, honey, coconut oil, and vanilla together in a medium bowl, mixing until smooth.
- Add flaxseed meal and protein powder of choice. Use a spoon to mix together it is too thick to stir, then use your hands to work it together. The goal is to have a cookie dough-like consistency.
- Press into an 8x4 inch pan (lightly greased or lined with parchment paper).
- Add dark chocolate to a small saucepan and melt on low heat until smooth.
- Pour the melted chocolate over the peanut butter layer and tilt the pan so that the chocolate covers the peanut butter layer entirely.
- Place in the fridge for 30 minutes to an hour before dividing into 10 bars or squares (or any desired shape).
- Store covered in the fridge for up to two weeks.

No-Bake Lemon Posset Tart

INGREDIENTS

 prep time: 20 min
 total time: 4 hrs
 servings: eight

Lemon cream filling:
- **Juice** and **Zest** from 3 lemons
- **3/4 cup** granulated Erythritol or Allulose (or alternative)
- 2 ½ cups heavy whipping cream
- **2 tsp** gelatin or agar powder
- **4 tbsp** water

Pie crust:
- **2 cups** whole almonds
- **¾ stick** unsalted butter
- **2 tbsp** powdered sweetener
- **½** vanilla bean powder **OR**
- **1 tsp** sugar-free vanilla extract
- **¼ tsp** sea salt, to taste

Pie topping (optional):
- **3** medium fresh strawberries
- **1 cup** fresh raspberries

Optional Garnish:
- Fresh mint leaves and/or powdered low-carb sweetener

Directions on next page.

DIRECTIONS

- Zest and juice the lemons. Set aside.
- Sprinkle gelatin into a bowl filled with 4 tbsp of water.
- Combine cream, sweetener and lemon zest in a saucepan. Gently heat just until it starts to simmer before adding the sweetener and gelatin, stirring until dissolved.
- Remove from the heat and set aside. Cover with a lid and sit for 10 to 15 minutes.
- Pour the now lemon-infused cream through a fine sieve and discard the zest. Stir in the lemon juice and set aside to cool down to room temperature.
- While that is cooling, place almonds, butter, powdered sweetener, vanilla and salt into a food processor. Process until the texture is sand-like.
- Transfer the dough into a 9-inch pie pan (removable bottom if possible) lightly greased or lined with parchment paper.
- Use your hand to firmly press the dough down the bottom and around the sides to create a slight edge for your crust. You need approximately 1 ½ inch crust to hold the filling.
- Place in the freezer for 15 to 20 minutes.
- Once the crust is set, pour in the cooled lemon cream and carefully place in the fridge for 3 to 4 hours.
- Serve topped with fresh strawberries, raspberries and mint leaves, if desired.
- You can also dust with some powdered low-carb sweetener, if desired.

Lemon Cheesecake

INGREDIENTS

 prep time: 20 min
 total time: 4 hrs
 servings: eight

Base Layer:
- **1 cup** macadamia nuts, roasted
- **½ cup** blanched almonds, roasted
- **2 tbsp** powdered Allulose or Erythritol
- **2 tbsp** unsalted butter
- **1 tsp** sugar-free vanilla extract

Cheesecake layer:
- **2 ½ cups** heavy whipping cream, divided
- **500 g** full-fat cream cheese or mascarpone
- **¾ cup** powdered Allulose or Erythritol
- **½ cup** fresh lemon juice
- **Zest of 1 to 2** lemons, to taste
- **½ to 1** sliced lemon, for garnish

Directions on next page.

DIRECTIONS

- Process roasted nuts in a food processor until finely chopped.
- Add 2 tbsp sweetener, butter and vanilla and process until it combined.
- Press into an 8 or 9-inch springform pan lightly greased or lined with parchment paper. Place in the fridge while you make the cheesecake layer.
- In a medium bowl, add 2 cups of the heavy cream to a bowl (reserve the remaining ½ cup).
- Add the mascarpone (or cream cheese), remaining sweetener, lemon juice and lemon zest (or to taste).
- Add ¼ cup lemon juice to start, adding up to ½ cup if you like a bit more of a bite.
- Use a mixer to beat until smooth and creamy and pour on top of the chilled nut layer.
- Spread evenly and refrigerate at least 3 hours before serving.
- Beat the remaining ½ cup heavy cream until still peaks form.
- Transfer to a piping bag to pipe or spread the cream on top 1with a spatula.
- Slice the remaining lemon to decorate the top of the cheesecake for garnish, if desired.
- Serve immediately or chill for an hour.
- Store in the fridge up to 5 days.

INGREDIENTS

 prep time: 1 min    total time: 5 mins    servings: four

- **2 cups** heavy cream
- **14 oz** can condensed milk
- **½ cup** K2 edible cookie dough
- **¼ cup** chocolate chips
- **¼ tsp** Vanilla extract

Optional Ingredients:

- **2 cups** frozen avocados
- **¼ tsp** Peppermint extract

(Mint) Cookie Dough Ice Cream

DIRECTIONS

- **Note**: if you have an ice cream maker, combine all ingredients in that and follow your manufacturer's instructions.
- If you don't have an ice cream maker, be sure to have a freezer-friendly container or loaf pan on hand to place in the freezer while you prepare the ingredients.
- In a mixing bowl, add the heavy cream. Use a hand-mixer and beat the cream until soft peaks form.
- Add the condensed milk and beat together until thick and fluffy.
- Fold through the cookie dough and chocolate chips (or any other desired toppings).
- Transfer the mixture into the loaf pan, cover, and freeze for an hour.
- For a healthier alternative, try freezing avocados and blending with the condense milk, adding cream only as needed to reach desired consistency. Add a dash of peppermint extract and you have mint chocolate chip cookie dough 'ice cream'!

INGREDIENTS

 prep time: 2-5 min  total time: 5-7 mins  servings: one

- **1-2 tbsp** grassfed butter or ghee
- **1-2 tbsp** MCT Oil
- **1-½ cup** of your favorite coffee!

For a **protein packed** coffee add:
- **1 scoop** collagen peptides
- **1** egg yolk **OR**
- **1 tbsp** of protein powder
- (This recipe yields a slightly thicker texture, more like a latte)

Optional addons:
- Dash of cinnamon, cocoa powder, pumpkin spice, etc.

Bullet Proof Coffee

DIRECTIONS

- Brew your favorite cup of coffee as usual.
- Combine all ingredients in a blender and process until smooth. Take caution when blending the hot liquid. Blend for a few seconds before letting the hot air escape from the blender. Repeat until desired consistency is reached.
- Have fun getting creative with this one, by switching up coffee as well as the other ingredients you add!

INGREDIENTS

 prep time: 2 min    total time: 5 mins    servings: one

- **1 cup** unsweetened almond milk (or alternative)
- **¼** avocado, sliced and frozen
- **1-2 tbsp** almond butter (can sub any nut or seed butter)
- **1 heaping tbsp** greek yogurt of choice
- **½ cup** ice
- **2 tbsp** sweetener of choice
- **2 tbsp** cocoa powder
- **¼ cup** K2 friendly chocolate protein powder (optional)

Chocolate Shake

DIRECTIONS

- Pour ½ cup of milk, almond butter (or another nut/seed butter), sweetener, yogurt and ice into a blender.
- Add your desired mix-ins and pour the remaining milk over the top.
- Blend until desired consistency is reached, add more milk for a thinner smoothie.
- If adding protein powder, you will need additional milk.

Tip: Sunflower seed butter is a great alternative for those with nut sensitivities - but always check the ingredients!

INGREDIENTS

 prep time: 2 min    total time: 5 mins    servings: one

- **1 cup** unsweetened almond milk (or preferred milk)
- **¼ cup** frozen avocado
- **1 tbsp** Greek yogurt
- **½ cup** ice
- **¼ tsp** vanilla extract
- **2 tbsp** preferred sweetener
- **¼ cup** fresh or frozen strawberries (or K2 friendly berry of choice)
- **¼ cup** vanilla protein powder (optional)
- **½** banana, (pre-sliced and frozen, optional)

Strawberry Vanilla Shake

DIRECTIONS

- In a high-speed blender, add half your milk.
- Add frozen avocado, Greek yogurt, granulated sweetener and ice.
- Add strawberries (or alternative) and pour the remaining milk over the top.
- Blend your shake until thick and creamy. For a thinner consistency, add more milk.
- If adding protein powder, you will need additional liquid of choice.

INGREDIENTS

 prep time: 2 min   total time: 5 mins    servings: one

- **1 cup** unsweetened almond milk (or alternative)
- **1-2 tbsp** almond butter can use any nut or seed butter
- **½ cup** ice
- **¼ tsp** vanilla extract
- **2 tbsp** sweetener of choice
- **¼ cup** frozen cauliflower or cauliflower rice (optional)
- **¼ cup** vanilla protein powder (optional)

Vanilla Protein Shake

DIRECTIONS

- In a high-speed blender, add half your milk.
- Add frozen avocado, Greek yogurt, granulated sweetener and ice.
- Add strawberries (or alternative), frozen cauliflower (optional) and pour the remaining milk over the top.
- Blend your shake until thick and creamy. For a thinner consistency, add more milk.
- If adding protein powder, you will need additional liquid of choice.

INGREDIENTS

 prep time: 2 min    total time: 5 mins    servings: one

- **1 cup** unsweetened almond milk
- **1-2 tbsp** almond butter can use any nut or seed butter
- **½ cup** ice
- **¼ tsp** vanilla extract
- **2 tbsp** sweetener of choice
- **¼ cup** frozen blueberries
- **¼ cup** vanilla protein powder (optional)

Blueberry Protein Shake

DIRECTIONS

- In a high-speed blender, add half of the milk, almond butter (or alternative), sweetener and ice. Add your flavor mix-ins and pour the remaining milk over the top.
- Blend your shake until thick and creamy. For a thinner consistency, add more milk.
- If adding protein powder, you will need additional milk.

INGREDIENTS

 prep time: 2 min   total time: 5 mins    servings: one

- **1 cup** unsweetened almond milk (or alternative)
- **1-2 tbsp** almond butter (can sub any nut or seed butter)
- **½ cup** ice
- **¼ tsp** vanilla extract
- **2 tbsp** sweetener of choice
- **1 tbsp** cinnamon
- **¼ cup** frozen cauliflower or cauliflower rice

Optional garnish:

- **¼ cup** vanilla protein powder
- Cinnamon stick for garnish

Cinnamon Shake

DIRECTIONS

- In a high-speed blender, add half your milk. Add your almond butter (or another nut/seed butter), granulated sweetener and ice. Add your flavor mix-ins and pour the remaining milk over the top.
- Blend your shake until thick and creamy. For a thinner consistency, add more milk.
- If adding protein powder, you will need additional milk.
- **Optional**: sprinkle cinnamon and/or add a cinnamon stick for garnish.

INGREDIENTS

 prep time: 2 min   total time: 5 mins  servings: two

- **2 cups** baby spinach, fresh or frozen
- **1 ½ cup** unsweetened almond milk (or alternative)
- **½ green apple**
- **¼ cup** chopped cucumber
- **½ cup** frozen avocado chunks
- **2 tbsp** hemp seeds
- **3 drops** Monkfruit Extract
- Optional: ice cubes

Spinach Green Smoothie

DIRECTIONS

- Pour half of the milk into a blender, or just enough to cover the blades.
- Add the rest of the ingredients and blend until smooth.
- Adjust the thickness of the smoothie by adding less or more almond milk.
- If the smoothie is too thick, add a tbsp of almond milk and blend. If too runny, add a few ice cubes.
- Divide between two large glasses and drink immediately.
- Can substitute an alternative sweetener if you don't have Monkfruit extract.

Summary

I truly hope you have enjoyed this book, and that it was able to assist you in learning about the new and improved K2 diet.

By adding more fats from unsaturated sources like nuts and seeds as well as increasing your intake of low-carb, high-fiber vegetables, you'll see benefits to your health, mental clarity and weight management.

If you are someone who has always been hesitant to try the keto diet but were turned off by the strict rules – K2 is the one for you! The next step is to start implementing the strategies into your daily routine. Start slowly and figure out what works best for you. You have all the necessary information to get started (and over 100 recipes to make your own! Wishing you all the best on your K2 journey!

Printed in Poland
by Amazon Fulfillment
Poland Sp. z o.o., Wrocław
01 November 2023

ed023aca-3ffa-4283-9ffa-f9d703a0e4ccR01